FOLKL
of Somerset

Revd Alan L. Holt at work in his study

FOLKLORE
of Somerset

Alan L. Holt

All the author's profits from this book are donated to
St Margaret's Somerset Hospice in Taunton

ALAN SUTTON

First published in the United Kingdom in 1992 by
Alan Sutton Publishing Limited
Phoenix Mill · Far Thrupp · Stroud · Gloucestershire

First published in the United States of America in 1992 by
Alan Sutton Publishing Inc · Wolfeboro Falls · NH 03896–0848

British Library Cataloguing in Publication Data

Holt, Alan L.
Folklore of Somerset
I. Title
398.209423

ISBN 0-7509-0221-3

Typeset in 11/14 Sabon.
Typesetting and origination by
Alan Sutton Publishing Limited.
Printed in Great Britain by
The Bath Press, Avon.

To My Wife
with grateful affection
after almost fifty years
of married life.

Contents

List of Illustrations

Preface

I walked into my garden the other day and gazed on a magnificent array of daffodils, crowded together in sheltered places, which had taken over from the displays of snowdrop and crocus. The magnolia tree was in full bloom, the hawthorn hedges and the horse-chestnut trees were beginning to come to life again, and I thought to myself that this was Somerset in miniature. What a glorious county! What other county can compare with Somerset for sheer beauty? Indeed, is there any other county that can boast four ranges of hills? The austere Mendips and the undulating red-soiled Quantocks, where the wild red deer roam and Samuel Taylor Coleridge, Sir Henry Newbolt and Wordsworth used to walk. Even the low-lying Poldens which overlook the Somerset Levels and the Plain of Sedgemoor have their charm, while the expanse of the Brendon Hills and the common present a landscape of spectacular beauty. Somerset in its loveliness – and still I have not taken into consideration the varied world of Exmoor, Cheddar Gorge, Burrington Combe and Wookey Hole. What magnificent grandeur these have to offer.

Yet it was while thinking of these things that I suddenly remembered a statement of Sherlock Holmes in his story *Copper Beeches*. He was travelling by train from London to Winchester with his friend Dr Watson to help a lady in great distress. As he gazed out of the window and saw the beauty of the countryside, and the lonely clusters of houses here and there, he said, 'It is my belief, Watson, founded upon my experience, that the lowest and vilest alleys in London do not present a more dreadful record of sin than does the smiling and beautiful countryside.'

Of course, even in lovely Somerset, there are no longer lonely and isolated villages such as Sherlock Holmes gazed upon, but there is no doubt that it is from these isolated communities that stories of folklore have their origin.

In the seventeenth century it is perfectly true that the parishioners in one small Somerset village boiled their vicar in a cauldron. In another village finger-marks of blood were left on the window of a manor-house which later revealed a body below the foundations. A flickering light on lonely Exmoor revealed a child's body which had been thrown into a well by her drunken father who could not afford, so he said, to pay 2s. 6d. to lodge her at Mrs Marley's house. There was a gibbet that stood for one hundred years on the lonely Quantocks. . . .

Yes, there is a host of weird, uncanny, strange, unbelievable stories in this book that I hope you will enjoy reading in the same measure that I have enjoyed collecting them and putting them into print.

Alan L. Holt April 1992
Lympsham
Somerset

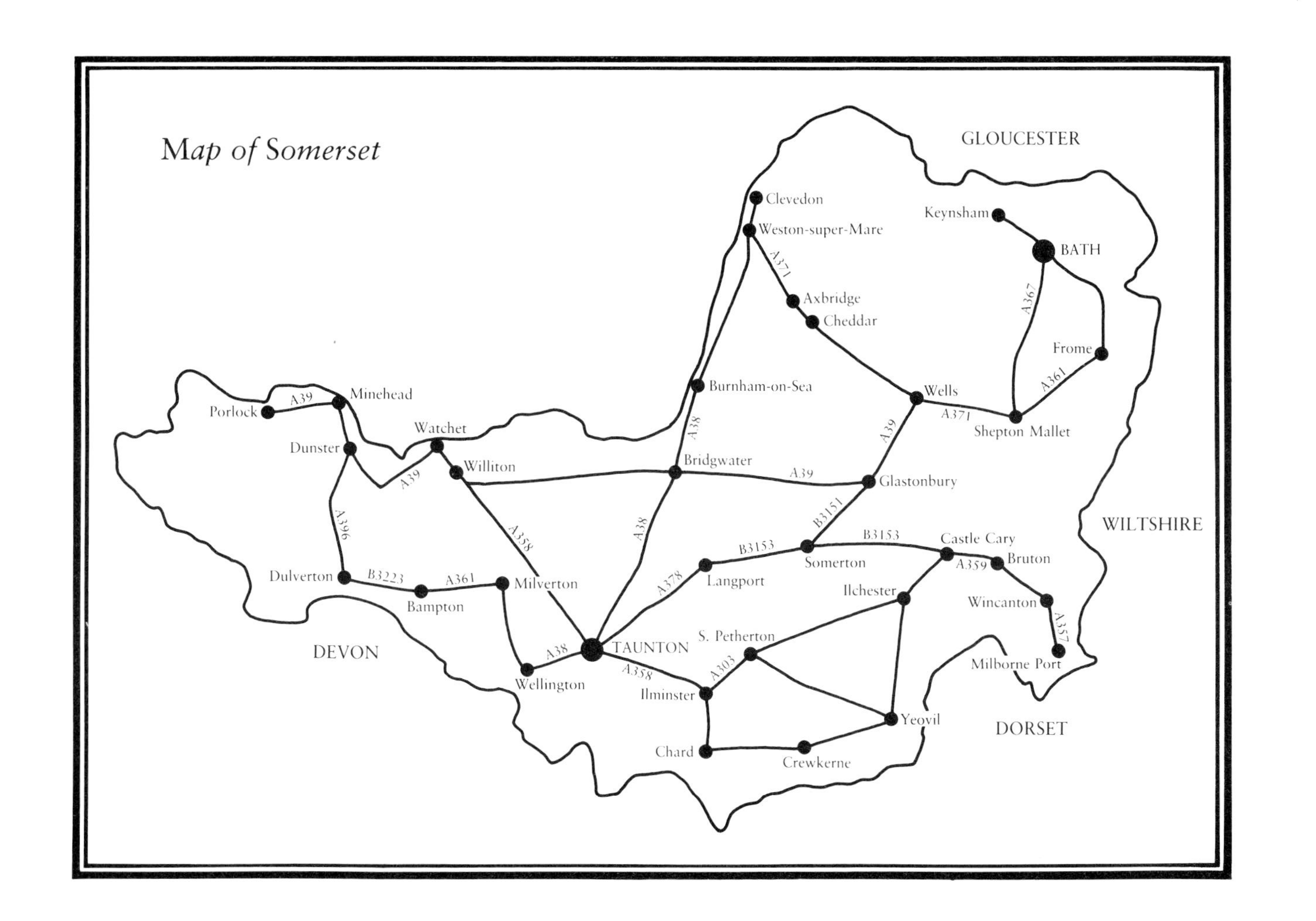
Map of Somerset
GLOUCESTER
WILTSHIRE
DORSET
DEVON
Clevedon
Weston-super-Mare
Keynsham
BATH
Axbridge
Cheddar
Frome
Burnham-on-Sea
Wells
Shepton Mallet
Porlock
Minehead
Watchet
Dunster
Williton
Bridgwater
Glastonbury
Somerton
Castle Cary
Bruton
Langport
Ilchester
Wincanton
Dulverton
Bampton
Milverton
TAUNTON
S. Petherton
Milborne Port
Wellington
Ilminster
Yeovil
Chard
Crewkerne
A39
A38
A371
A367
A361
A396
A358
B3151
B3153
B3223
A378
A359
A357
A303

1: A Case of Murder

The Boiled Vicar. The Conibeer Family. The Reservoir. Merland'sCorner. Murder Lane. Whistling Copse.

The Boiled Vicar

Old Cleeve is a lovely, sequestered village within four miles of Minehead, although it lies hidden from the main A39 road. It boasts a church some 500 years old, and in the churchyard there is a gravestone in memory of George Jones, a village blacksmith of 1808. The epitaph reads:

My sledge and hammer lie reclined,
My bellows too have lost their wind;
My fire's extinct, my forge decayed,
And in the dust my body's laid;
My coal is burnt, my iron's gone,
My nails are drove, my work is done.

Here was a soul who seemed to have reached his end, and was quite content to lay down his tools of office calmly and serenely. We can almost picture him doing it.

How fortunate such men are, for I am afraid all men do not come to the end of life's journey in such a lovely way. Take the case of the Revd Mr Trat who went as curate to the Revd Edward Brickenden, rector of Old Cleeve.

Now, there is a tendency for us, in the twentieth century, to believe the present age to be a most permissive one. But I can assure you that the beginning of the seventeenth century was not an age either when citizens stood rigidly by the Ten Commandments, or even by the law of the land. Mr Trat, however, was one who did believe in adhering to the Ten Commandments, and was convinced that everyone else should do likewise. Whatever he declared from the pulpit, he believed, was the 'Word of the Lord', and should be obeyed.

Owing to the fact that he was somewhat outspoken in the pulpit there were people in his congregation who were convinced that he knew more about them than they wished him to know. The cap seemed to fit. In fact, he provoked them to such an extent that they did all in their power to discredit him in both the eyes of the Law, and in the minds of the hierarchy of the Church.

For instance, one of his adversaries impersonated the curate by walking the highways wearing a similar cap and gown to those worn by Mr Trat. At night the impersonator would accost women, who would then complain to the magistrates, but under cross-examination their only rather unconvincing evidence was the description of Trat's cap and gown.

When Trat's wife was cut off by the tide near Blue Anchor and was unfortunately drowned, his adversaries suggested that he was the cause of her death. As all these allegations proved baseless it became obvious to his enemies that some other way had to be found to cut off the head, and cut out the tongue, of this successor of John the Baptist. Although they did not have a King Herod, nor an Herodias to help them they did have a Peter Smethwick. When Peter Smethwick, the grandson of the rector of Old Cleeve, became aware that his relative, the Revd Edward Brickenden, was about to resign the living, that was bad enough. But when he later gathered that the perpetual patronage of Old Cleeve had been sold to Trat, which in the past had been promised to him, it was the last straw, for it meant that Trat could stay in Old Cleeve forever.

Smethwick now began to lay his plans in deadly earnest and with the utmost care. He brought to his assistance Andrew Baker, Cyril Austen and Alice Walker. When Trat was out on his horse, visiting his parishioners in his far-flung parish, the three men, who had been hiding in a ditch, sprang upon him, dragged him from his horse, and unmercifully stabbed him to death.

The Revd Mr Trat was now dead and would never speak again, which is exactly what Herodias believed when she had asked for the head of John the Baptist. But just as she was wrong, so Smethwick and his murderous gang had not yet heard the last of the Revd Trat.

It was not until the vile deed had been perpetrated that the murderers realized they had to answer the one question that every murderer throughout the ages has had to answer. How does one dispose of the body? To murder was simple. It was the disposal of the body that created problems.

The three men came to the conclusion that they would take the body to Trat's own home, since, from the death of his wife, he had lived there by himself. There they severed his head and tried to cremate it. Having cut off his legs and arms, they then proceeded to disembowel him. Then they put the bowels into earthenware pots. Finally they put the body into a container, and after filling it with water and salt, left it for Alice Walker to boil. But even when they had completed this deliberate process they still found that there were remains they could not dispose of. However, with the head gone, and the other parts dismembered, they were convinced that no one could ever prove the dead man's identity.

Now what should they do? All they could do was to wait . . . and they didn't have to wait long. Within two weeks Trat's disappearance had been reported to the police, who found it expedient to break into Trat's home, where they found the dismembered remains. The three men had decided that if this did happen, and for some reason they themselves were asked questions by the police, they would offer the suggestion that the dismembered remains must be that of a beggar whom Trat had murdered in a fit of temper. To confirm this report, Peter Smethwick's father again played the role of impersonator. He rode through the village and elsewhere, even as far away as Devon, dressed in Trat's cap and gown. And it is quite probable that this deception could have worked. Only one thing stood in the way. The police had found Peter Smethwick's coat in the curate's house. What was it doing there?

The police made exhaustive enquiries, and Alice Walker was the first to come under suspicion, and was detained. They then came across charred pieces of skull bone and a pot full of blood. When the police asked Andrew Baker to hold it he accidentally dropped it to the ground, convincing them that he was not innocent of the crime. In consequence both he and Peter Smethwick were detained. Cyril Austen, who made good his escape by fleeing from the village, was eventually found miles away, but with a piece of blood-stained cloth still in his pocket. Lastly, the itinerant roving impersonator was added to the bunch of evil-doers.

Peter Smethwick, Alice Walker, Andrew Baker and Cyril Austen were found guilty of murder. Although they never confessed their guilt, it did not save them from the gallows. They received their deserts on the morning of 25 July 1604, when they were hanged from Stonegallows, immediately west of Taunton. The elder Smethwick, the impersonator, was sent to gaol to await further evidence against him, but whether he was hanged or not, I do not know.

Many people have told me that when they walk from Old Cleeve to Blue Anchor they often hear footsteps on the road, and yet when they stop to ascertain who is following them, they see and hear nothing. It is believed by some that those footsteps belong to the elder Smethwick, who still strides through Old Cleeve and Chapel Cleeve all by himself.

Sometimes they hear the footsteps late at night, when good Christian and law-abiding citizens should be asleep in their beds.

The Conibeer Family

Not far from Old Cleeve is another much smaller village by the name of Woodford. This village or hamlet is on the B3190 to Bampton in Devon.

In 1775 there lived, in an old Jacobean house, an 88-year-old lady by the name of Elizabeth Conibeer and her two daughters, Anne, aged forty-five and Sarah, forty-three. On 5 June, having finished their midday meal, the three sat together waiting for the baker's boy to arrive. They had the money ready for him on the kitchen table, but history will show that that money was never paid.

The ladies may have thought that the footsteps they heard sometime later were those of the baker's boy, but they were wrong. The footsteps belonged to someone else, and no one has ever been able to say with conviction whose footsteps they were; what the person looked like; or what he wanted. In all probability we can assume he did not want the money, for, when investigations began, the few coppers for the baker's boy still remained on the kitchen table. Of course, in deference to this argument it could be said that the baker's boy might have disturbed the murderer at his task, the latter fleeing before he had time to take the money. As the boy was too cautious to go back to the scene of the crime, the money remained on the kitchen table. No one knows. But the memory of the baker boy's experience must have been carried with him to the grave. The results of the savagery and brutality which he saw could surely only have been executed by someone with a deranged mind. It was either that, or the very devil himself had called on the Conibeers that day.

The boy saw before his incredulous eyes three women huddled on the floor in a pool of blood. Elizabeth, the old lady of eighty-eight, lay on the kitchen floor with blood oozing from her throat and side, while Anne lay on one side of the table and Sarah on the other, slashed to pieces. It is said that blood was everywhere: on the floor, table, chairs, fireplace and even the crockery. Again, it was not congealed blood that the boy saw, but blood that was still oozing from the bodies and running on to the floor, leaving only one conclusion to be drawn. The boy must have arrived soon after the dastardly deed had been perpetrated.

At the same time he must have been a brave lad for he did not give way and collapse. Although horrified to such an extent that he left the door half ajar, he rushed away as fast as he could to raise the alarm. It may have been a good thing for him that he did, for in all probability the monster could still have been in the kitchen holding the knife ready to commit another crime if he thought it essential for him to do so.

No one seems to know who it was who carried out this dastardly crime. No one to this day has been able to come forward with an answer. Surely it could not have been a total stranger or a psychopath out to murder defenceless women, for if so, why did the murders begin and finish here at the Conibeer's house in Woodford? From what we can gather there was no rumour or suspicion pointing to anyone in the vicinity, and certainly no one ever confessed to the murder. Furthermore, there appeared to be no motive.

All we know for certain is that the Conibeers were buried in Monksilver's churchyard, because the tombstone still stands, on which we can plainly read the following:

> In Memory of Mrs Elizabeth Conibeer aged Eighty Eight years. And her Two daughters Anne aged Forty five and Sarah Forty three who was all inhumanly Murdered in the Day of the 5th June 1775 in their House in Woodford in this Parish.

Inhuman wretch, who e'er thou art
That didst commit this Hainous crime
Repent before thou dust depart
To meet thine Awful Judge Divine.

The Reservoir

Durleigh is a fascinating village near Bridgwater where, I suppose, apart from the church, the most interesting place is West Bower Farm. In its earlier days, when West Bower Farm was known as the Manor, it belonged to the Seymours and was probably the house where Jane Seymour was born. She was the only wife of King Henry VIII with whom he found no fault, for she bore him a son, who later became King Edward VI.

The Seymours would not have known Durleigh reservoir, which now adds distinction to West Bower Farm, for it was not constructed until four centuries after their time. Sometime before the reservoir was completed, a very peculiar and mysterious event happened in Durleigh.

Next to the well-known West Bower Farm, although some distance down the road, stood a small isolated cottage which had probably belonged to a neighbouring farm in the village in days gone by. This attractive cottage had been sold to a couple who were both strangers to Somerset and therefore knew nothing at all of Durleigh or its environs, which made people question why they ever came to live there. However, they seemed a perfectly devoted couple, living happily on their own in their cottage in the shelter of the valley. The owner, Ben Stoddard, a rather refined and always immaculately dressed gentleman, kept himself much to himself and seemed rather older than his very beautiful wife Betty.

Although the cottage was small it was elegantly and tastefully furnished and decorated, giving the impression that the

Stoddards were not only refined and educated but were also undoubtedly endowed with abundant blessings of this life. For instance, they could afford to employ a local and handsome young man by the name of Michael Abbotts to tend the garden, horses and stables, and a maid, Grace Burton, to clean the house and prepare their meals. The cottage was delightfully situated, directly facing the rough red-stone church, which had been built in the thirteenth century in a part of the Royal Forest of North Petherton, perhaps a mile across the valley, where the good-looking Michael Abbotts lived. For a year or two the villagers frequently remarked on the obvious happiness of the Stoddards for they were constantly seen together, either riding in their trap, walking alongside the valley, or shopping together in Bridgwater. Hardly was one ever seen without the other. Yet the people of Durleigh considered them something of an enigma.

After the space of some two to three years their habits began to change. Ben and Betty were at times seen on their own, Ben driving his horse and trap or riding his favourite stallion, while Betty was frequently seen walking alone in the evening down in the valley between the church and her home. This change of attitude on the part of the Stoddards was so noticeable that it gave the villagers a lot to talk about, for not much went on in Durleigh unnoticed by its inhabitants. Grace Burton said the change was markedly pronounced. Not only, as she subsequently remarked, were they often now seen on their own, but she had frequently heard them quarrelling violently in their home. On one or two occasions during their quarrels she had heard her master refer to Michael Abbotts.

Probably unknown to Grace Burton, people in the village were beginning to whisper that there was something going on between Michael Abbotts and Betty Stoddard, although they had to admit, when questioned, that the two had never been seen together. Grace had hardly ever seen them talking with one another, in the cottage or even in the garden. Most of the conversation concerning the garden, which was of a considerable size, was carried on between Michael and his employer, who seemed to be on remarkably good terms with one another. However, all the whispering came to a head early one morning when Frank Staple, being late for work, was taking a short cut across the valley. To his horror he saw Betty Stoddard lying on her back with her eyes and mouth wide open, with congealed blood on her forehead, hair and neck, some of which had run into her eyes. He did not have to look twice to know that she was dead.

It instantly appeared to him that Betty had been dead for some time, and this, too, was the coroner's verdict. In fact it was later confirmed that she had died at about 10 o'clock the previous evening. But how did she die? This was the question everyone in Durleigh had on their lips. She must either have been bludgeoned by a heavy blow from a weighty instrument, or she must have stumbled and landed on an upturned rock when attempting to negotiate a sheer, but insignificant, drop of some 15 ft. Certainly the huge rock beside her body and upon which part of her body was resting was spattered with blood. Here was a mystery indeed . . . and many people, who had little or no knowledge at all of the facts, came to their own preconceived conclusions.

It was said that there were definite footmarks all the way from the Stoddards' cottage, which stopped at the spot where the body was discovered, while the same footmarks were seen pointing in the direction of the cottage. Certainly someone had walked from the cottage and back again not many days before . . . and those footsteps were too large for a lady. It was also asked why Stoddard had not raised the alarm himself when his wife failed to return home that night. There was no doubt, they said, that Ben Stoddard had murdered his wife after discovering, by some means or other, that there was something going on between her and Michael Abbotts, and on that fateful night Stoddard had followed her soon after she had left the cottage for her lone walk down into the valley. It was all supposition, however, and the coroner came to another conclusion. He considered he said, from all the evidence afforded him, that her death was one of misadventure. But the rumours persisted.

The other cause for suspicion was that immediately after the inquest Ben Stoddard left Durleigh overnight, and for good. He was never seen again. His departure may have been brought about by the persistent and ugly rumours spread about him which could not have possibly escaped his attention. But in his defence, his hurried departure may have been caused by the fact that the valley was in the process of being flooded to construct a reservoir, which necessitated many buildings in the area being demolished, including part of West Bower Farm itself. But so far as we know Ben Stoddard did not even wait for his compensation.

In a season of great drought, the lines of hedgerows, undulations and the foundations of buildings can still be seen on the bed of the lake. But that is all that can be seen. One can no longer see the supposed footmarks of Ben Stoddard, or the huge rock which was responsible for Betty's death. The reservoir alone hides the mystery. Today, home to wild birds and numerous trout which give sport to hundreds of ornithologists and anglers, the reservoir covers the land where ploughmen once ploughed, and cornlands once flourished and Betty Stoddard once walked, when the sun set over the Quantock Hills. All is now changed.

Merland's Corner

I remember, many years ago now when I was a much younger man, walking all the way from Taunton, the county town of Somerset, to Churchstanton, an isolated village resting beneath the Blackdown Hills. Part of the latter part of the journey still stands out in my mind, even today, for I remember so well how captivated I was by the changing colours of the leaves in the woodlands, the undulating slopes of the hills and the absolute quietness of the lanes. I also realized, by the time I reached Churchstanton, how tired and hungry I had become.

As the local inn had not yet opened I timidly knocked on the door and asked whether mine host would serve me a pot of tea and a few sandwiches. A coal, peaty fire smouldering in the grate, coupled with the humid atmosphere of the room and the tiredness of my body, soon overwhelmed me and I fell asleep. I awoke only when someone entered the room and smilingly asked me how far I had travelled that day and from what direction I had come. When I told him I had walked from Taunton, he said, 'So you must have passed Merland's Corner, then?' I told him I had no idea what he meant by Merland's Corner. He then took a long draught of beer, and coming nearer to me said he would tell me a true story concerning that bend in the road which had always been called Merland's Corner.

'Once upon a time,' he said, 'out there, on those hills there lived alone a gentleman about whom it had always been rumoured he had lots of money, which was one of the reasons,' he put his finger to his mouth and whispered, 'he always kept himself to himself. One day a big, stray, white dog came to old John's house, and although he advertised it far and wide, no one ever claimed it, while the villagers said they had never heard of a white dog being in the village before that time. In due course the dog, now called Merland, and old John became inseparable.

'Soon after this, a gentleman, who many subsequently thought could have been old John's brother, was seen in Churchstanton almost daily, but from where he came no one seemed to know.

'Now it was on an evening such as this, still and overcast, that a sense of foreboding enveloped the village. It was an uncanny feeling. It was so quiet that to everyone the change in atmosphere, and the sudden change in temperature, appeared unreal.

'Early the next morning, as Harry Peck was on his way to milking, he saw someone lying by the side of the road. Beside the prostrate form, a big white dog was striding up and down, quietly, yet having a wildness in its eyes, that although Harry was on horseback, he dare not approach the body with the dog nearby. Never had he seen a tame dog with such wildness in its eyes. From the bottom of its throat proceeded a continual rolling, guttural growl, which seemed like one continuous cry from the underworld. Although Harry had always had much to do with animals he had never heard or seen anything like this before.

'For a moment he was rooted to the spot, quite incapable of knowing how to react to the situation, but then recovering slowly, he urged his horse forward and galloped to the farm to bring back five or six herdsmen to help him keep the dog at bay. The unbelievable sight which met Harry as he alighted from his horse stunned him. He had, in his time, felled an ox with one or two blows, but old John had received eight to ten gashes in his head by blows far mightier than ever he could have inflicted. Furthermore, they were inflicted by a heavy object, from which the first blow must have rendered death instantaneous.

'By now a few more people had arrived from the farm, and recognizing the dead man, ran to the lonely home where old John had lived as long as any of them could remember. They found the house in a state of chaos: sheets were stripped from the bed; coal and peat lay on the drawing-room carpet; drawers had been turned upside-down and their contents strewn over the floor; floor-boards were raised from their joists and walls broken in. It was a scene of complete disorder.

'There was no doubt that someone had heard of John's supposed wealth and had come to find the hoard, but whether they had been successful, or whether John even had any money, remains a mystery to this day. But although old John had been murdered he was certainly not murdered in his house, for there was not a speck of blood to be seen. But the most curious aspect of the murder was how could old John have been murdered or the house ransacked if Merland had been on guard?

'There seemed to be only one feasible explanation, and that was that the house was ransacked at night by someone who knew that old John took a late night's walk with Merland immediately before retiring to bed. And John must have arrived home the moment his adversary had left. Many believed that that adversary was John's brother, who they had seen walking in the village lately, for how could a stranger know whether or not he was a wealthy man? Certainly the person who had ransacked John's home was looking for something. Now a man who has had riches one moment, must find it extremely hard to be penniless the next, and this is what must have struck John when he saw his home had been rifled. If he had had money, he now knew that his wealth had gone, and by God, he was not going to lose it easily. And if he had no money he wanted to get hold of the man who had ransacked his house.

'Rushing out of the house as fast as his legs could carry him, he did not give a moment's thought to the consequences. Just at the end of the road, he was pounced on from behind and was bashed on the head eight to ten times by a heavy, blunt instrument. Leaving his victim on the ground, the adversary rushed off with all haste, never to be seen again.

'No one can explain how it was that old John could have been attacked with Merland by his side unless, of course, Merland knew the culprit as a friend. Was that friend old John's brother? The only alternative is that the dog could have been in two minds, whether to chase and hold his man, or try and help his master by staying at his side . . . at the side of the man who had taken him in, when others refused to own him.

'There is one further mystery concerning the murder. No one seems to know what happened to either Merland or the murderer after that night. All we do know is that every now and again, a phantom white dog is seen at that corner, and sometimes a long muffled howling is heard far into the night. Even to this day that bend in the road at Churchstanton is called 'Merland's Corner' or 'Murderer's Corner'. Even they who do not believe in ghosts, have to admit that when they walk round Merland's Corner at night they experience a sort of creepy feeling . . . a feeling that they are not alone . . . and that the unseen company is not a pleasant companion.'

Murder Lane

I wonder how many of you know or have ever heard of Baltonsborough in Somerset which stands in a marsh on the banks of the River Brue. Yet it was in this small village that St Dunstan was born: a man of rare distinction upon whom the choicest gifts of body and mind were bestowed. It has been said he was a true artist, accomplished in metal work and in music and a man of beauty and attractive manners with a deep religious conviction. No wonder then, that in AD 940 King Edmund appointed him Abbot of Glastonbury, and in the reign of Edgar the Peaceful he became Archbishop of Canterbury. A remarkable man, one of the foremost of English statesmen in his days, and he was born in the little known village of Baltonsborough.

But there was also another person born in Baltonsborough who had none of St Dunstan's charm and qualities. His name was William Rendell, and to learn something of this man we must go to Lottesham Green on the outskirts of

Baltonsborough. I warn you, however, never to go there after it is dark, for it is said someone in white walks silently down that lane and across the field directly facing the two semi-detached cottages. Sometimes, it is said, a faint cry is heard as though someone is plaintively pleading for help. At other times a low, murmuring sound is heard. Of course, there are those who consider this mere fanciful – yet the local people always refer to Kite Lane as Murder Lane, and I will tell you the reason.

In 1937 a horrible murder took place there, dreadful in its execution, and made more so in that it was carried out on one who was always believed to be as pure and undefiled as her name. In a semi-detached cottage in Murder Lane there lived a Mr and Mrs William Rendell. I suppose it would be fair to say that William was a farm labourer, but in no way did he have permanent employment and neither did he do all his work locally. His business was to go from farm to farm and village to village in search of work, coming home to his wife to stay a week or so when an odd job could be found in the village. But before long his restless spirit would set him off once again for other fields.

Mrs Rendell (maiden name, Lily Stickland), who owned the cottage in which they lived, was born in a neighbouring village and was therefore very well known to all and sundry, who unanimously declared her to be a loving, loyal woman of great moral fortitude. However, on one of his returns, the neighbours reported a violent quarrel between Lily and her husband during which William was heard to declare that his wife had been unfaithful and had been going out with someone else during his absence. This she stubbornly refuted. Her story was corroborated by everyone in Baltonsborough who had known Lily over the years. They knew her, they said, to be as pure as the driven snow.

Sometime after the vicious quarrel the neighbours, mystified by the silence next door and fearing something may have happened to one or other of the occupants, informed the police.

On entering the cottage, police officers found Lily covered in blood with her throat cut from ear to ear. It had been a brutal and diabolical murder and, although William could find no escape from the accusation, he did, under a sudden impulse, flee from the scene of the crime. Nevertheless it was not long before he was apprehended and brought to a charge of murder. On Wednesday 9 June 1937 William Rendell, the farm labourer of Kite Lane, Lottesham Green in Baltonsborough, was found guilty at Wells Assize and was sentenced to death.

I can never pass that little cottage in Kite Lane even today, or indeed pass the top of the lane itself, without thinking of charming little Lily and that beast of a man whose name was William. Who could believe that such a lovely little village could house so vile a wretch?

Whistling Copse

Just off the A39 Wells–Bath road, after leaving Corston, there is a village by the name of Newton St Loe. Near a big island within two miles of Bath there is a road running almost parallel with the A39 which leads to the village. The village itself was named after St Loe or the de Sancto Lando family, who not only once held the manor here, but also the manor of Corston. In the garden of the former are the ruins of a castle, where, it is believed, King John (1199–1216), who signed Magna Carta, was once held captive. Now, someone else in Newton St Loe was once held captive about whom I would like to tell you.

Near Newton St Loe, on the manorial estate, is a well-known wood known as Whistling Copse, not to be confused with Stantonbury Hill to the south-west, which is far more extensive. The name Whistling Copse suggests to the mind something secretive and mysterious. And indeed there was something enigmatic about it which had not escaped the notice of the owner. He was convinced that there was something mysterious, if not illegal, being committed within that extensive woodland. In fact, he was absolutely sure that someone was trespassing in that wood and he strongly disapproved of it, especially when he was shown that his annual bag of pheasants and partridges seemed to be decreasing at the same time as the costs for maintaining and expanding his game bird preserves were increasing rapidly. Something was happening down in Whistling Copse about which he wanted to know. With this in mind he issued definite orders to both his chief and assistant gamekeepers to be diligent and alert in their pursuit of trespassers or those who violated his premises.

One day, while walking the grounds, both gamekeepers, seeing pheasants taking wing for no apparent reason, went down to Whistling Copse to investigate. There they saw, much to their surprise, a poacher, seemingly without a care in the world, carrying a brace of pheasants in his hand. Creeping down behind some nettles they challenged the poacher to come forward. On that glorious day, when everything was still and quiet, for not much disturbs the peace and tranquillity of Newton St Loe, shots were heard echoing from Whistling Copse. The poacher, though hit and badly wounded, managed to get back to his home on the outskirts of Bath. But the chief gamekeeper lay dead in Whistling Copse.

With a witness to hand in the form of the assistant gamekeeper, the poacher was soon apprehended and was eventually sentenced to life imprisonment for murder. But the following year, for no apparent reason, the assistant gamekeeper committed suicide, leaving not one witness, apart from the prisoner, to tell of that fatal afternoon. And the prisoner had always strenuously maintained that he was innocent. Twenty years after his prison sentence the poacher was released but died a broken man soon after.

The question that is still to be asked is, did the poacher or anyone else actually commit murder . . . or was it an accident that caused the death of the gamekeeper? Many believe it to be the latter. The poacher never confessed to the crime and, in fact, denied it up to the day of his death. He maintained that when the gamekeeper made his challenge from behind the nettles, he himself fired two pellets into a tree in an endeavour to scare the gamekeeper off. That was all. He never aimed at the challenger at all, for he maintained he could not even see him.

Well then, was it murder, manslaughter or an accident? The argument still goes on in Newton St Loe and many of the villages round about. It is still a real 'hot potato', I am told, although the killing took place some sixty years ago. The only place from where we could gather the whole truth, if only trees could talk, would be Whistling Copse, but that lies still and peaceful on the side of the hill, guarding its own secrets.

Newton St Loe, where a murder took place in Whistling Copse. But who was the murderer?

2: *The Mysteries of* Ponds *and* Bogs

Popham's Pit. Pinkworthy Pond. Emborough Pond.
Mollie Phillips and the Rector of Cutcombe.

POPHAM'S PIT

Wellington, a town with a population of some 16,000 people, is situated in the south-west part of Somerset and only 3 miles from the borders of Devon. It was the conqueror of Napoleon who made the town famous although, it must be said, he did not accept the town of Wellington as his first choice and I think it is true to say he only visited it on one occasion. But there was another great man of Wellington who, although he was not so universally renowned as Wellington, was certainly well known wherever Englishmen resided. For it was he who was responsible for the execution of Guy Fawkes and Sir Walter Raleigh.

His name was Sir John Popham (1533–1607). He was educated at Balliol College, Oxford and admitted to the Middle Temple in 1550. He rose to be Lord Chief Justice in the reign of Queen Elizabeth I (1558–83) and was appointed Attorney-General in 1581. He was Crown Prosecutor or judge in many state trials including that of Mary, Queen of Scots, the conspirator Babington, Robert Campion the Jesuit, and he appeared as witness as well as judge in the trial of the Earl of Essex. It is

Sir John Popham

said at his death in 1607 he had the largest fortune ever amassed by a member of the English bar.

His most notable acquisition during his lifetime was the beautiful Littlecote estate and manor in the parish of Chilton Foliot on the River Kennet near Hungerford. This manor was made over to him by William 'Wild' Darell, which, in the eyes of the public, made the judge an extremely unpopular person. Here is the reason.

William 'Wild' Darell was a very rich, proud and reserved man but, owing to continual litigation with his neighbours and most of his relatives, his legendary crimes and his illicit love affairs, he was finally reduced to dire straits in spite of having inherited some twenty-four estates and manors at his father's death. One of the cases against 'Wild' Darell came before Judge Popham, which occasioned enormous interest in this county.

One night a midwife was visited at her home by a horseman dressed in a long black cloak and wearing a slouched hat which fully concealed his identity. She was asked whether she would do something for him without any questions being asked, for which, in return, she would be paid a very high price. To receive this sum she would have to be blindfolded and ride pillion. She consented. But while she was being escorted on a roundabout route she began to realize she had done something which she would find very hard to explain away. She asked herself why this secrecy was necessary if a crime was not being perpetrated and why she had to be blindfolded. But before she had time to answer these questions, the journey ended.

Unaware of the house or even the town to which she had been taken, she was swept from the horse and led into a bedchamber. There she was asked to deliver a mother of her child. In her capacity as midwife she was quite willing to do this and therefore consented. But imagine her horror, when she had delivered the child, to see it snatched from her arms and thrown without ceremony on to the fire. Although horrified, and now feeling very much afraid, the courageous woman, before being blindfolded again, was able to cut a piece of material from the curtains and still had the presence of mind to count the number of stairs as she descended to the ground floor.

On reaching her home, she went immediately to the magistrate and told him her story and, when the house and the room had been finally identified, 'Wild' Darell was arrested and charged with the murder. Darell was subsequently tried before Sir John Popham . . . and acquitted. This acquittal aroused widespread anger in circumstances made worse by Darell's surrender of Littlecote Manor to the judge, which, as the majority of people believed, had been given as a bribe to save his life.

Be that as it may, William Darell remained 'wild' to the very end. When he surrendered Littlecote Manor to Sir John it is said he cursed him personally and subsequently placed this curse on the family, that the latter would perish in the male line. Both these curses seemed to have the desired effect, for the Popham family has ceased to exist and Judge Popham himself reached his end in a very dramatic and disastrous way. There is a story, well authenticated, that while hunting beyond Wellington the judge was thrown from his horse and his body lost in a bog. This bog, it has been suggested, was a bottomless pit on the Blackdown Hills, well known today as 'Popham's Pit' or 'Wilscombe Bottom', from which, it is believed, his remains were never extricated.

The tomb of Sir John and his wife Amy, who died at Wellington in 1612, is a prominent feature in Wellington church, standing at the east end of the north aisle. The judge is wearing his black robes, his golden chain of office and his square black cap. His coat of arms is painted on the canopy set above him on eight black columns. But does the judge lie there? Or is he in the bottomless pit outside the town? Hundreds believe the latter to be true. Indeed, when his tomb was moved into its present position in 1938 it is said that remains purporting to be those of Lady Popham were found, but those of Sir John were missing.

Perhaps he still lies in 'Popham's Pit' as legend has it, despite the inscription on the monument which reads:

> Sir John Popham, Knighte and Lord Chief Justice of England and of the Honourable Privie Counsell of Queen Elizabeth and after to King James. Aged 76, died 10th day of June, 1607 and is here interred.

Is he interred here? I wonder.

PINKWORTHY POND

When John Knight of Worcester bought the Royal Forest of Exmoor, as it had been known over the centuries, his first great work was to wall in the whole of his estate, some 29 miles in all. He then began to build roads from Exford to Simonsbath and South Molton as a means of transporting produce to and from Simonsbath and to encourage people to settle in the vicinity. This was indeed a sensible thing to do and one could understand why he encouraged such work. But it has always been a mystery why he should have imported gangs of Irish labourers to construct such a monstrous thing as Pinkworthy Pond (known locally as Pinkery Pond). This pond was some 7 acres in extent and some 30 ft deep. It was constructed near the Chains on Exmoor, a large remote area, one of the loneliest and most frightening places in the whole of the county. It is almost as eerie during the day as it is at night.

There are no lights up there at night-time and when the moon is shining it seems to give it an even more ghost-like appearance than when it is hidden behind the clouds. I do not believe that there can be a lonelier spot anywhere on Exmoor or in the county itself. Deer never seem to visit it, and I can't remember ever having seen an animal of any kind anywhere near. It is a lonely and oppressive place. I have often wondered why it had always had such a depressing power over man – what it was that gave it such a sombre and funereal aspect – until I learned a little of its history.

The pond itself is in the shape of an imperfect triangle, curving somewhat at the north-west and wandering away a little at the north-east. The 7 acres of water fills a depression which, as I have remarked, Irishmen dug in the time of John Knight. But why he wanted to build it at all, or to build it in such a desolate place, no one seems to know. The water can sparkle on a bright day, which is typical of so many lakes, but the peaty bottom of

Pinkworthy Pond, near the Chains on Exmoor. To this day the pond retains the mystery of a supposed suicide victim, whose body was never found

Pinkworthy Pond gives it an almost continual blackness that drives away even the animals. If we wish to approach this desolate spot we will be able to keep ourselves dry by staying as close as possible to the wall, but we will have problems if we proceed along its marshy hollows, just where the River Exe begins to rise. It is remarkable, is it not, that the Exe, that lovely sparkling river wherein trout abound and which runs gaily through the county of Somerset, begins here, in these peaty, dank and dark uplands. Yet no one should ever go to Exmoor without visiting the Chains and Pinkworthy Pond, for otherwise they have not really seen Exmoor. But they should not go alone and they must also see that they are not up there when the clouds are low or night is setting in. The warning has been given.

There is no wonder that in this lonely, isolated spot in 1880 a young farmer, at the nadir of his life, decided that there he must end his days. Nothing up there could prevent a would-be suicide doing otherwise. The hat and coat of the missing man were found on the bank and when dragging did not uncover the body, the age-old device of 'a lighted candle floating on a loaf' was tried. But the wind is nearly always too strong up Pinkworthy way to allow a candle to remain alight, and the loaf failed to come to rest over the corpse, the belief being that it should. Even divers failed to find the body, so thick and inky is the water. The body was found only after the pond had been drained. It was emptied again in 1913 in search of another suspected suicide, but nothing was ever found and Pinkworthy retains its mystery.

This surely must be one of the reasons why Pinkworthy Pond has such a depressing power over man. It is believed that this suspected suicide still walks the Chains by day as well as night. Sometimes when we think the whistling we hear up there is caused by the wind blowing through the openings in the walls, it is well to look around and see whether the reeds are also blowing. And if they are not, then it is not the wind that has caused the whistling. And if it is not the wind that caused the whistling, we must ask ourselves . . . what did?

Emborough Pond

The village of Emborough, a few miles from Shepton Mallet and Wells, seems to have an air of sadness about it and even the thirteenth-century church (now redundant) in no way lifts our hearts. The exterior looks bleak at the edge of the fields, while the interior speaks far too much of death. I counted something like twenty of the Heppisley family alone, buried there in the church. But not only is it sombre within the church, Collinson, the renowned Somerset historian, had to admit that Emborough Pond and its surrounds were also gloomy. He referred to the pond as 'a dismal sheet of water', bordering the main road and flooding an area of something like 10 acres. Emborough Pond has also been referred to as a crater of a volcano, because 'no one seems to know its origin', and also because there are many who consider it to be a bottomless pit. I will tell you why.

Years ago, there lived on the borders of Emborough, so I was told when visiting the area on one occasion, a young gentleman who captivated most of the young ladies living in the area and beyond. His name was John Roger, an infrequent visitor to the village, for he had been away to a public school and had only recently finished his time at a university. 'If my memory serves me right,' said the old man who was telling me this story, 'he was the son of John Thomas Leach, one of the owners of the coal-mines in the district.'

John Roger was a handsome young man, tall, athletic and full of vigour. At the same time he was something of an intellectual, ambitious, honest and, what we would call today, a young man of sterling qualities. He was always in his place at church on Sundays during the vacations and the rector thought much of him. However, away from school and the university, there was little to occupy his time in Emborough, apart from the occasional social evening and a day now and again with the local hunt . . . and then there was Emma.

Now Emma was one of the maids at the manor-house in the vicinity. She was an attractive little thing, with a good sense of fun, given to too much giggling, which annoyed John's finer tastes. However, he could forgive her for this, for she was such a good sport who brought so much gaiety to his life. Before long, John found himself falling in love with her, and there was no doubt she was madly in love with him. It wouldn't do and he knew it. He was well aware his parents would object, but what was the alternative? He told himself over and over again that his parents would never hear of such a thing and moreover, if ever they got to know he was associating with her, he would probably be driven from home. As a consequence the parents would see to it that Emma too was driven from the manor. In her love for John, Emma was too trusting a girl to think that he would ever tell her a lie or abandon her. But, although John loved her and meant to marry her when he obtained his articles, he was not wholly speaking the truth when he told her he was not dependent on those at home for his livelihood. On one occasion, when they had made arrangements to meet, Emma had to let him down for she was not feeling too well. In fact, she had not felt well for some weeks and she wished her mother was alive to help her. She dare not say a word to anyone else, not even the other maids at the manor . . . and her father, she thought, would be no help to her at all. She was growing weary and impatient with things and more than annoyed that she and John had not met for some time because of her indisposition.

But it was all the happier when they did meet. They walked for a long time through the woods; up hill and down dale, while laughing and joking and holding hands. She was blissfully happy when she was with him, and felt so secure with him by her side. Moreover, she was not too timid to tell him so, for her buoyant spirit could not possibly keep her thoughts or her feelings to herself. And he, likewise, was radiantly happy as they sat together on an old fallen log. After a time he stood up and went away to pick some bluebells for her but, looking at her from a distance as he came slowly back to present the flowers, he was convinced she looked bigger than usual. Stopping abruptly in his steps, pretending to smell the bluebells, he took a longer look.

'She is pregnant,' he said to himself, 'there is no disguising it.' Surely that was what the villagers had been saying when they suddenly stopped talking as he went into the village shop recently. What a fool he had been not to realize it. Why didn't she say something about her condition to him? Why hadn't she told him? 'Surely she knew she couldn't possibly hide it forever,' he murmured to himself.

He didn't say much to her as they wended their way home for he could sense she was radiantly happy and he did not wish to make her otherwise. But their happiness was not to last for long. He kissed her as he said 'good night' at her father's cottage that evening. After she had entered he stayed awhile wondering whether he ought to go in and tell her father he was responsible. But before he could make up his mind he could hear the two arguing fiercely inside. He heard the crashing of furniture, the breaking of crockery, Emma screaming and a man shouting. He now shrank from going in and, paralysed with fear, clung to the shadows. He heard the door open. Then he saw Emma rush out, run down the narrow street, and into the front door of a cottage where John knew her granny lived. Within a few moments her father rushed out, still brandishing his belt, and swearing and shouting enough to stir every household in the vicinity.

When all was quiet, a disconsolate John began to walk home. Would he encounter a similar home-coming? He knew he was responsible for Emma's condition. He also knew he had lied to her when he told her he was not dependent upon those at home for his livelihood. He was caught in a trap and did not quite know how to extricate himself. Luckily they were all out when he arrived home for he felt that if Emma's father knew, then his parents may have found out likewise. He quickly went to bed only to have a very fitful night.

The dawn came with violent consequences. The word had been noised abroad in no uncertain manner and the Leachs were about the last in the village to know, which made the situation worse. It was a day of violence when John was at the butt-end of punches, vitriolic attacks, unpleasantness from brothers and sisters, hostility from father and even enmity from mother. What could and should he do? Obviously as long as he lived in Emborough he would suffer the consequences.

After two weeks of insufferable bitterness he went out one night and knocked at the door of the house where Emma's granny lived. He had to see Emma again, to comfort her, to tell her of his eternal love for her, and that he would wait to marry her if only she would do likewise. But before he could say all that was in his heart, he heard Emma's father stamping in through the front door as though he knew he was there. At that moment John went noiselessly out at the back.

John did not go home that night, nor the next, nor the next. On the eighth day of his disappearance a jacket was found by Emborough Pond which his parents stated categorically belonged to John. In fact, a scrap of paper in the top breast pocket, proved them to be right. But where was their son? Drowned? Well, footmarks had been seen which seemed to suggest that John had been near the pond at sometime. Within a few days a handkerchief was found floating by the water on which were stitches J.R.L. which Mrs Leach knew she had stitched with her own loving hands. But although the pond was dragged day after day, John Roger was never found.

'Well, of course not,' said the old man of the village, 'I knew they'd never find anyone there . . . the pond has no bottom to it. No one has ever touched bottom in there.'

Emma lost her baby and stayed for a while with her granny in Emborough until all murmuring and whispering had ceased, and then went to Axminster in Devon to a dear, old friend of the family by the name of Mollie Cotton. When Mollie died Emma found that she had been left the cottage.

Some years after John's disappearance a postman, who had left Emborough at about the time of the great scandal but who knew nothing about it, returned to see his sister who had been taken ill. When he was told of John's disappearance he said, 'You know . . . I delivered to the Leach's home about that time what appeared to me to be a very important letter. It was marked 'Private' and had an Australian stamp on the front and an armorial bearing on the flap of the envelope, and it was addressed to J.R. Leach, Esq., BA.'

Did John go to Australia? Did he drown himself in Emborough Pond or did he accidentally fall in? We can only answer two queries with regard to this story. The first is that Emma never married; the other is that the mystery is still unsolved. As for John he was never heard of again.

A shiver always runs through me when I head due west along the B3114 road towards Chewton Mendip and look back over the village of Emborough. I cannot get out of my mind poor Emma in that house with her father. No wonder she lost her baby. And I often wonder whether she ever came back to look across Emborough Pond and if she did, whether she shed a tear. I also wonder whether she ever forgave John. I think she did, for few other couples could have loved each other more passionately than they.

Mollie Phillips and the Rector of Cutcombe

From whatever direction we approach Exford we have to descend into it. In the valley a bridge takes us over the River Exe which, coupled with the fair expanse of village green, makes it a delightful oasis on a summer's day. There is a smithy in the village who appears to be as busy as when one depended solely on the horse for transport. Of course, we have to remember we are at the centre of activity so far as the Devon and Somerset Staghounds are concerned. On the right hand side of the road that leads to Simonsbath are the stables of the D & S Staghounds and further up the hill on our right are the kennels. They were all built by Mr Mordaunt Fenwick Bisset who was Master of the Hounds from 1855 to 1880 and who was, apparently, one of the best masters in the history of the hunt. But even in such a lovely place as Exford the macabre is wont to come to the surface every now and again.

On Sunday 8 September 1929, Mollie Phillips, who worked for Mr Leslie Tucker of Rocks Farm, Exford, told Annie Rawle, the housekeeper, that she was going to Cutcombe to visit her aunt, Mrs White. She added that she would be back in the evening to lock up the chickens. Mollie Phillips, however, never arrived at Mrs White's house; neither did she return to lock up the chickens; nor did she return to Rocks Cottage where she lived. This small, pleasant young lady, standing only about 5 ft 3 in tall, had vanished . . . into oblivion.

Of course, hundreds of other unhappy and frustrated girls have left their homes to find fortunes elsewhere, but in most cases the parents have some idea as to the reason. But Mollie was happy at home. This was a case, so far as one can tell, of a perfectly happy country girl vanishing into thin air without a cause. And so far as we know she had no boy-friend. Hunts were organized; volunteer parties were led by the police; the army joined in the search, covering acres of moorland, commons and woodlands. Ponds were emptied, rivers searched, but Mollie Phillips was nowhere to be found, dead or alive.

However, on Friday 27 March eighteen months after Mollie's disappearance, Donald Grant of Hawkington Farm was on Codsend Moor, near Dunkery Beacon, when he saw, protruding from a spring of water in boggy ground, a human skull and the bare bones of a body. Here were the remains of Mollie Phillips and the search for her ended. But the questions concerning her disappearance were by no means at an end. For instance, how did she come to her end? Why was she on Codsend Moor? Why was she, and her clothing, not found months earlier? Had she been murdered and, if so, by whom? Had she been caught in a bog? But are bogs in that region so perilous?

In evidence, Donald Grant described the place where the body was found as more of a spring than a bog. Certainly no harm had ever come to his animals. If Mollie had kept to the pathway which led from gate to gate across the moor he could not possibly see how she could have been sucked in by the supposed bog. Conversely Jack Pugsley, a rabbit-catcher, said he had, in his time, been in the bog as deep as his thigh. From such conflicting evidence it was very difficult indeed to arrive at any definite conclusion.

Dr Godfrey Carter, the pathologist, said, after examining the body, that he found no fractured bones or obvious signs of injury or assault. He believed the cause of death was shock and exposure with the possibility of final drowning. He was certain she was not dumped into the bog, but may have fallen into it while running. But why was she running? Had she been inveigled on to the moor, and then bolted in terror trying to avoid her pursuer or whoever it may have been? Another puzzling feature in this case was that a stone, weighing some 30 lb was found pressing against her body. What was it doing there?

We have to remember that the area around Codsend had been scoured by scores of people soon after Mollie's disappearance. Yet she was not found for eighteen months. Was it that someone had dumped the body there after the commotion had died down, placing it in position by this heavy weight? This theory would disagree with Dr Carter's findings, but it was feasible. After all the evidence had been given, the coroner, Mr Geoffrey Clarke, concluded by informing the jury that they could return one of three verdicts: wilful murder; misadventure; or an open verdict. Within a very short time the jury had agreed on a verdict of misadventure, although they did add a rider that Mollie Phillips had been hurrying away in fright from some person who was not necessarily near her.

This was not a very conclusive verdict and the rector of Cutcombe, the Revd Arthur Courtenay Jenoure was quick to see it. He had been rector of Cutcombe since 1923, and his six to seven years' experience had told him a great deal about Codsend and Mollie Phillips. He said in the pulpit at Mollie's funeral that he considered a jury of twelve-year-old schoolboys could have come to a better verdict. To ask those who knew the girl to believe that her death was due to misadventure is to offer the greatest insult to their intelligence, he said. So disgusted was he with the verdict that he said he was prepared to let anyone throw him into Codsend bog and, if he failed to get out within five minutes, he would contribute £20 to charity, providing the challenger doubled the money. The rector of Cutcombe was not to be easily placated. His campaign encouraged other people to come forward: a resident of Tiverton had seen a man struggling with a girl on the slopes of Dunkery Beacon on the day of Mollie's disappearance. A man from Wales spoke of a dream he had had of a man quarrelling so violently with a girl that he strangled her before dragging her up the side of the hill and dumping her into a swamp. In fact, Mollie Phillips' disappearance caused such a stir that it encouraged Mr Lovat Frazer, MP, to ask Mr Clynes, the Home Secretary in the House of Commons, whether he proposed to take any further action in the case.

But then, just at the point when interest was beginning to die down and it was felt the case would never be re-opened, especially as Mollie's mother did not desire it, some hair, believed to have belonged to Mollie was found . . . on Codsend Moor. Here was a climax indeed. On this occasion Sir Bernard Spilsbury, the renowned pathologist, was brought into the case and asked to examine the hair.

The national press, the country, Exford and the rector of Cutcombe waited anxiously for news. The Mollie Phillip's case was the subject of everyone's conversation. Even the D & S Staghounds had to take second place until the result of the examination was reported. In due course Sir Bernard reported that, 'the almost absence of roots shows that the hair was not torn from the head as it may have been had there been a struggle. The appearances were consistent with the hair having been bitten off by an animal such as a fox or dog.' He went on, 'The fact that the girl's spectacles were found near the skull indicates that she was wearing them, and supports the view that she was alive when she entered the bog.'

The case was ended. The report of Sir Bernard Spilsbury closed the case as nothing else could. It also caused the deputy chief constable to say that the police had never found any evidence of foul play and 'we therefore arrived at the conclusion which has now been confirmed by the most skilled pathologist in the land.' But the rector of Cutcombe said, 'The case is not dead; it is very much alive.'

So what did happen? Did Mollie come to her own death in a bog on lonely Codsend? Why was she there when she had intimated that she was going to see her aunt? Had she previously arranged to meet someone on the moor but told Annie Rawle she was going to see her aunt to avoid suspicion? Did someone kill her and dump her body in the bog holding it down with a 30 lb weight until the water's persistent running loosened the stone, allowing her body to rise to the surface? Or did someone terrify her and, in running away, did she fall into the bog and drown? If so, was the person who terrified her the murderer? And if so . . . where is he now? As the rector in that little village of Cutcombe said, 'The case is very much alive.' The mystery is still unsolved.

3: *Prophecies and Portents*

The Dove of Bardon House. The Flickering Light. The Lighted Cottage. The Curse of Loxton.

THE DOVE OF BARDON HOUSE

Within half a mile of Washford on the A39 Bridgwater – Minehead road are crossroads, easily recognizable by the radio station close by, with masts some 700 ft high. To the right of the crossroads is Watchet on the coast, while to the left is

Bardon House, once mysteriously haunted by a white dove said to be the embodiment of Mary, Queen of Scots

Wiveliscombe in Somerset and Bampton in Devon. Within a mile, on the right hand side of the road to Wiveliscombe, is a great avenue of Spanish chestnut trees. This avenue of trees, which leads to a very old and extremely quaint building known as Bardon House, is all that is left of some 70 acres of timbered woodlands, mostly Spanish chestnut trees. The house is in the parish of St Decumen's, Watchet, whose church can be seen on the hill to the right of the A39 road. And it was to this house that Robert Leigh and his family came from Devon in about 1595.

Now, to understand the following historical and interesting story I have to say, first of all, that Robert Leigh's godfather was Robert Scudamore who was under-Secretary of State to Queen Elizabeth I towards the end of the sixteenth century. And it was because of this that the quaint old house, in this out-of-the-way corner of north-west Somerset, had a connection with the eventual execution of Mary, Queen of Scots in 1587.

I first ventured through that avenue of trees leading to Bardon House in the evening when, although it was not dark, so closely knit were the trees that the sunlight could hardly pierce the foliage. There was such a distinct sense of loneliness and eerieness about the place that, had a dark figure passed in front of me, I would not have been surprised. But nothing did pass that evening, although it is said that the ghost of Robert Leigh still haunts the avenue, and I can well believe it.

As I began to drive slowly forward I eventually saw a dim light at the end of the tunnel and then, passing into sunlight, the quaint old Bardon House presented itself. There are stories concerning Bardon House which chill the blood. It is said an old lady with white hair and dressed in black is often seen about the passages in the dark, and sometimes a harpsichord is heard being played at the dead of night. But how true these stories are I cannot tell. But our real interest lies elsewhere. There was an attic in the gable over the drawing-room in Bardon House whose only light came from a small window.

We are told of a white dove that repeatedly flew towards that window, sometimes with such force as to shatter the glass to fragments. Each time the window was mended the white ministrant returned to break it once again. This was a mystery that went unsolved for many, many years.

The Leigh family had been residents in Bardon House for decades, but in 1830 William Leigh, a solicitor, became its owner. Very soon he began asking questions of his maids and local folk as to the rare behaviour of the dove. Surely it could not be the same dove? But not being able to placate the dove, nor quell the stories surrounding it, he eventually decided to have the attic completely cleared. In due course a small parcel was found, upon which were written the following five words: 'Concerning the Queen of Scottes'. The parcel was opened and therein were papers, now known as the Bardon Papers, which threw another light on the interesting transaction in our history concerning the trial of Queen Elizabeth I's secretary, the conspirator Babington, and the eventual trial of Mary, Queen of Scots and her execution the following year.

In 1844 William Leigh died and the Bardon Papers appear to have been placed aside again. However, in 1870 these papers were again brought forward and were eventually sold to the British Museum where they can still be seen. They are catalogued, 'Egerton Manuscripts 2124'. It is thought that the papers at one time belonged to Sir Christopher Hatton, Lord Chancellor and mouthpiece of Queen Elizabeth in the House of Commons in 1587. Undoubtedly he collected these papers to prepare the speech when Parliament was especially summoned to take measures concerning Mary in 1586. And there seems to be no doubt that Scudamore, Robert Leigh's godfather, must have brought these papers to his godson at Bardon soon after 1595 when they were deposited in the small attic and presumably forgotten.

But what of the dove that caused the attic to be cleared? Well, many people refer to the white dove as the embodiment of

Mary, Queen of Scots. Certainly it is true that since the parcel was opened and placed in the British Museum, the window in that small attic has never been broken by doves again. The mystery remains as to why it was thought necessary to have broken it before, for surely Mary, Queen of Scots was dead and finding a parcel could not bring the poor soul back to life? But whatever the connection, it seems quite remarkable that such a small out-of-the-way place in Somerset should have connections with Elizabeth, Queen of England, and Mary, Queen of Scots.

The Flickering Light

In a book called *Reminiscences of an old Country Clergyman*, the author, the Revd W.H. Thornton, has many delightful tales to tell. But the Revd Mr Thornton was not only a writer, he was also a great reader of character and an able administrator. He was also the first rector of Simonsbath.

I once had the privilege of being allowed to park my caravan in a very lonely part of that village, near to an old farmhouse which the farmer's wife told me was haunted. She had no doubt about that whatsoever. And I can believe it, because there are places on Exmoor so eerie and frightening they are beyond man's comprehension. I must say I was pleased I had the farmhouse, haunted or not, beside me for although there may have been a ghost lurking in the house, there was also the farmer and his wife who gave me courage. I remember on one very black night, looking out of my caravan window trying to understand why bright lights occasionally appeared on the horizon and instantly disappeared. My wife and I eventually discovered they were car lights which were seen on top of a hill but then disappeared as the car began to descend behind a vast crop of trees. That question had now been answered satisfactorily. But we never did discover what caused the blue light to flicker in the valley near where my caravan rested and where we knew it was quite impossible for any car to approach. It was only on recalling the incident some time later that I was told the following true story.

If we enter a gate beyond the River Barle immediately opposite Simonsbath Lodge we will eventually come to a beechwood where, if we forked right, we would find ourselves in a sunken lane. On the left is a strange mound known as Flaxbarrow beyond which is a ruined cottage. Beside this cottage are some old mine workings known as the Wheal Eliza which were opened in the days of Frederick Knight. Lower down, on the banks of one of the tributaries of the River Barle known as the White Water, there once stood a cottage inhabited by William Burgess, his wife and three children, Tom, Emma and Anna. In 1857 Burgess's wife died and Burgess, with his three children, went into lodgings at the home of Mrs Marley at Simonsbath. Very soon afterwards Burgess sent Tom and Emma into service on a farm, but kept Anna in lodgings with himself.

One Sunday in June, 1858, Burgess told Mrs Marley he was taking his daughter Anna to live with her grandmother at Porlock Weir, and he returned the same day without the chid. But during the days that followed some burnt clothing was found at the back of Mrs Marley's home which she was convinced had once belonged to little Anna and, as Burgess was no longer living at the home of Mrs Marley, suspicions were immediately aroused. Not least disturbed was the vicar, the Revd W.H. Thornton, the first vicar of Simonsbath, who had been deceived by Burgess before. He therefore asked William Court if he would go to Porlock Weir and, without arousing suspicion, ask a few questions of Anna's grandmother. Very soon he was able to report that Burgess did visit her on the Sunday, but he had no child with him.

Now it was the custom, when sheep stealing abounded, for thieves to bury their booty until they could dispose of the carcass and apparently someone had done this near the mine workings of the Wheal Eliza. Some sheep thieves had noticed a small mound in the ground and, assuming they had found a dead sheep or two, asked Burgess to remove the carcass for which he would be given a good reward. But there were no sheep in that mound near the Wheal Eliza; it was little Anna's body . . . and Burgess knew he was cornered.

He now had to move the body, deposit it in a place where he was convinced no one would ever find it, and then leave the area as quickly as possible. But the fact that he disappeared at the same time as Anna's burnt clothing was found aroused suspicions as nothing else could, and it was not many days before he was arrested in Swansea. When asked where he had disposed of his daughter's body, Burgess remained silent and was consequently locked up in Dulverton's gaol. However, when two months had passed by without any more convincing proof having been brought against him the magistrates of Dulverton came to the conclusion that they could hold their man no longer. But at this vital point in the proceedings two things came the way of the searchers.

The first one was that many local people maintained they had seen a mysterious flickering blue light hovering over the shaft of the Wheal Eliza, a sign, they were convinced, that Anna's body was somewhere in the vicinity. There was also another rumour being spread abroad concerning a man who had told the vicar that he was down by the Wheal Eliza one night, soon after the disappearance of Anna, when he had seen someone moving from the direction of the empty grave to the Wheal Eliza pit shaft.

On the basis of these two rumours Thornton immediately informed the magistrates at Dulverton who proceeded to have the shaft cleared of water, a process which took some three months. When most of the water had been pumped out, a young man volunteered to go down the shaft. When he resurfaced he held in his arms a tarpaulin parcel. The vicar opened it and there lay little Anna, clothed in a little cotton dress . . . but nothing was left of her face. The vicar's last work in this macabre affair was to bury the poor little soul in his own churchyard. Later, Burgess confessed his guilt, saying he had murdered his daughter as he could no longer afford the 2s. 6d. a week which it cost him to lodge her at Mrs Marley's house. He was hanged publicly at Taunton Gaol on 4 January 1859.

But was it the man's evidence that caused the Wheal Eliza shaft to be investigated, or was it the flickering blue light which the local people said rested over the shaft? Before we dismiss it too lightly, some people insist that the same light still flickers there today.

THE LIGHTED COTTAGE

I was once driving along the A30 Yeovil – Crewkerne road when I noticed a signpost directing me to Haselbury Plucknett. I immediately turned in that direction because I was convinced I had once heard that St Wulfric the Hermit, or St Ulrice the Recluse as he was also known, once lived there. I also remembered that, in days gone by, he was a sufficiently compelling person to prompt the King of England, King Henry I, to go to him for advice. I was pleased I had seen the sign for I found my suppositions to be true. The hermit, St Wulfric, did once live in a solitary cell in Haselbury Plucknett.

Before he had lived in the village very long the impression produced on the popular mind by his self-incarceration was considerable. As his body wasted, so his fame grew, until he was hailed all over England as a miracle worker and a prophet. He was visited by thousands of people who sought counsel and consolation and was, as mentioned above, visited by King Henry I and Stephen. To the former he foretold his death; to the latter he prophesied that he would become King although he was not, at that time, in line to the throne.

Wulfric died on 20 February 1154 in his ninety-first year. He was buried in the church of St Michael in Haselbury Plucknett where his tomb was visited by hosts of pilgrims from far and wide. It was while I was visiting this church, specifically to learn more about St Wulfric, that a sudden storm prompted me to call in at the White Horse Inn, now the Haselbury Inn, for something to eat and drink. Before long as is usual I find, I was approached by someone who I subsequently learned was one of the oldest men in the village. By devious means, and in a very short time, he had learned that I was interested in the folklore of Somerset and he was anxious to tell me of an incident that his grandfather had told him about when he was a child.

'I was about twelve years old when my grandfather, one stormy night, told me the following tale in this very place in which we are now sitting. My grandfather said, "I remember one November, leaving the White Horse Inn in Haselbury Plucknett to walk to Misterton on a very beastly night. Had my wife not expected me home I do not suppose I should have been such a fool as to have attempted the journey in such conditions. The rain was pouring down, and although I had started out well protected, before very long the rain was shooting down my neck in torrents. The journey would have been made easier had not the wind been blowing a gale, but both elements, it seemed, were doing their utmost to make my journey as uncomfortable as possible. I can never remember such a night. The rhines, which had already been full before the storm, were now overflowing and pouring on to the hard surface, making a quagmire of even the best roads. By the time I had covered half my journey I was so wet that it would not have been advantageous for me to turn back, and I was aware that I would be able to reach Misterton with an extra, determined effort. I must admit that I frequently felt like getting into a barn and sleeping away the night, but that would have been foolish in my present sodden state.

"It was at one of these junctures, when I felt that I could neither go forward nor return, that I saw a light in the distance piercing the seemingly impenetrable darkness. I could see neither a star in the sky, nor the outline of a building, nor even the trees. All was thick and desolate darkness apart from this light which seemed a mile away but which must have been much nearer. I therefore hurried forward as fast as my sodden covering would allow me and I saw the light came from what I had always considered to be a disused cottage or small farmhouse. Here, surely, I said to myself, was shelter of some sort, and I approached it optimistically, thinking that a hot cup of tea or cocoa would rejuvenate and warm my weary and wet body. I knocked timidly on the door, for it was late at night and I did not want to wake anyone from a deep sleep, but no one came in response to my knock. Having knocked once more to no avail, I wondered if I should leave the cottage in peace and go on and complete my journey. But at that moment a cold shiver ran through me which determined me to try the door. Silently I pushed it open and walked in with my heart in my mouth for by now I was beginning to feel there was something uncanny about the place. The temperature of my body had now changed to a burning throbbing caused by an irregular and thumping heartbeat. Only a really conscious effort on my part prevented me from swooning.

"Inside the door was a narrow passage with a door at the further end from where a shaft of light gleamed. For some inexplicable reason I walked stealthily and silently in the direction of that shaft of light. I knew I was trespassing and had no right to be there but, at the same time, no one was answering my call and I was now anxious to know the reason. On reaching the door I knocked again, slightly harder than before. Surely someone must have been inside, I said to myself, otherwise there would be no light and the doors would not be unlocked. But still no one came and so I pushed the door as I had done the other, which opened at the slightest touch. This was uncanny! It was frightening! It was weird! But then, and nothing could describe my thoughts or my immediate reactions, I saw there was no furniture or anything else inside the room apart from an old man and a woman. They stood there, looking out of the window . . . oblivious to me . . . oblivious to my knocks . . . oblivious to everything. Surely both of them could not be deaf!

"'Good evening,' I said, 'I have been caught in the storm and have yet a few miles to go. I wonder if you could offer me a cup of tea or cocoa or something to warm me before I continue. I would be pleased to reward you.'

"I said this without any conscious thought, for I realized afterwards that without furniture of any kind, it was very doubtful whether they had any means for making tea, even if they had a supply. Receiving no reply I cautiously approached them but in doing so noticed there was no fire in the grate, on such a terrible night as this. There was hardly any glass in the window against which they were standing and yet it seemed to make no difference to them. I also noticed that although the wind was blowing a gale through the window, their hair did not even shimmer in the wind. It was only then that I came to my senses and realized that I was in the presence of the paranormal and, as I was wondering what to do under such circumstances, the figures before me vanished, as did the light. For some inconceivable reason I ran from the house as fast as my crumbling legs could carry me. Before I had travelled far I was once more back into impenetrable darkness, and, looking back, I no longer saw the light which had attracted me to the cottage.

"I do not remember getting into bed that night or even arriving home, but I do know that when I awoke next morning my wife was sitting on my bed proffering me a hot cup of tea. It was the nicest cup of tea I had ever tasted. I drank it down and must have sunk back to sleep immediately, for it was evening before I once more returned to consciousness.

"Although I felt I would be laughed at if I recounted my experiences I could in no way keep them to myself, so you may imagine my surprise when no one seemed to reject my story as I thought they might. I was later told by a gentleman, who was a local historian, that my story had been corroborated repeatedly which prompted him to fill in the background to my experiences. I was told that down a lane where the River Parrett crosses the A30, undoubtedly the place where I had seen the apparition, there was once a small farmhouse where Zechariah Parson lived with his wife and daughter Rose, whom they loved dearly. Although Rose was their only daughter, theirs was not a possessive love for when Rose told them she was to marry James Berkeley, they were overjoyed and began to make immediate preparations for the wedding. The Parsons and the Berkeleys were well acquainted for both had been farmers in the locality for very many years and both families were known over a wide area. There was no doubt about the wedding being a tremendous affair.

"However, there is many a slip between the cup and the lip. One day when riding with the local hunt, James met with a fatal accident when his horse failed to make a simple obstacle and he was thrown headlong into a bank and broke his neck. It was James Berkeley's father who broke the news to the Parson family the next day whereupon Rose, clasping her hands together, cried, 'Oh, not my James', and fell senseless to the ground. From that moment the girl never worked again. She did not help her mother in the home; she did not clean her room or lay her bed; she did not even go to the market; and the only people she would meet were the Berkeleys. She seemed to lack enthusiasm for anything. Many people thought her parents should have made her do something, or they should have spoken harshly to her, or reproved her for her laziness. Truly these friends may have been right, but the parents were beside themselves wondering what they should do for the best. They were hopeful, they said, that she would change as the months went by.

"One winter's night, when it was very cold, rain was falling and the wind was blowing a gale, Rose told her parents she would like to go and see the Berkeleys. They tried to persuade her not to go out on such a blustery night by consoling her as best they could. Eventually they gave her a warm drink and took her to bed. That was the first time Rose's parents had ever refused her anything, and it was to be the last. In the morning she was missing. Her mother said she thought she had heard some movement in the night, but fooled herself it was the wind. Rose's body was later found floating in the river Parrett.

"It was now the parents' turn to become depressed. After the loss of their daughter, they avoided all social intercourse. They kept themselves to themselves and it was only possible to learn about them and their activities from relatives after Rose's funeral. Apparently they did not live for many years after Rose's death. However, for months and months, especially during the winter or during a storm, they would spend most of their time looking out of the window as if expecting their daughter to return, and it is said they never locked the doors.

"No one lived at the house after their death and it gradually fell into disrepair. Yet to this day, so it is said, a light is seen coming from the ruin of the cottage where once the Parsons lived. And many people have told me that they have seen Zechariah Parson and his wife looking out of the window as they have passed by in the night. They are easily visible, they say, for when they stand in the window there is always a light in the room with them."'

The Curse of Loxton

There are two very steep hills beside the M5 motorway between Bridgwater and Weston-super-Mare. The one on the left is Brent Knoll and the one on the right is Crook Peak. Lying between these two landmarks are two villages. One is Christon, boasting a Norman church, and the other is Loxton.

When I was walking through the village of Christon I spoke to a lady, a resident, who told me, in the course of conversation, how proud she was of her village, the Norman church and, more especially, she said, of the village's hospitality. 'It has always been this way,' she said with some fervour, 'even from the days when the Romans came.' I couldn't understand this statement at all. 'You see,' the lady hurried on, 'when the Romans came this way, the people of Christon welcomed them with open arms, whereas the people in Loxton, down the road, refused them hospitality. As a result,' she told me, 'the Romans cursed the village of Loxton and the curse has been on it ever since. I would never go to live in Loxton. None of us would,' she said. This statement fascinated me and, as I could not understand it, my investigations began in real earnest.

Loxton was once a little known hamlet nestling under the Mendip Hills between Bleadon and Compton Bishop until Gerard Tiarks became its rector in 1875. He was so keen on hunting that very soon the small hamlet became well known to huntsmen near and far. The big house, which apparently juts out into the road in the centre of the village, was built by the rector and the building on the opposite side, on the hillside, was built as his hunting lodge. Gerard Tiarks, it must be said, was a hunting parson in every sense of the word. But he was still a parson. It is said on one occasion he was riding alongside a member of the hunt when the latter's horse threw him into the rhine where he was submerged by the water. When he eventually surfaced the huntsman looked up meekly at the parson and said, 'I didn't swear, did I parson?' Gerard replied, 'I didn't hear you, I must admit, but there were some uncommonly large bubbles coming to the surface.'

Gerard Tiarcks had three nephews, Herman, Frank and Harry. In the year 1900 Herman, who later wrote a colourful book called *Hunting Reminiscences*, went to live at Webbington Farm, which his father owned, where they both hunted with the Weston and Wells Harriers. During this period they were successful in building new kennels, and later, for four seasons, Herman had the honour of being Master of the Mendip Harriers. Up to this moment all seemed to be going well with the Tiarck family, but very soon there was to be a marked change.

Herman's brother Harry, of the 5th Dragoon Guards, who had taught Herman 'how to jump gates', died of enteric fever. Herman's own hunting days were finished on 26 May 1936 when he was thrown from his horse, badly kicked and suffered three broken ribs and concussion. Later, his wife, who didn't learn to ride until she was twenty-one, died of tuberculosis. Frank's son, Edward Peter, died in a flying accident in 1929 and later Frank's wife Emmie died in the natural course of events. But Frank endured no other misfortune up to the time of his death in 1952. However, people who had been closely associated with Frank were now in grave trouble. To understand this better let us go back a few years.

When Frank and Emmie lived at the lodge, two other ladies, a Miss Maria Buls, Emmie's companion, and a Miss Noreen O'Connor, who regarded the Tiarcks with almost idolatrous respect, lived with them. Everyone with whom I have spoken has told me of the good work Noreen did, not only as a companion to the Tiarcks but also in the village itself. She loved and helped her church, she sat on every committee in the village and worked untiringly for all concerned. When the extension to the village hall was first mooted Noreen offered her services in every field of activity. However, after the death of

Emmie and Frank in 1952, Noreen and Maria left the lodge, the home of the Tiarcks, and went to live at Gardeen, a house further down the road.

On 2 September 1954, the whole village and locality were aghast to hear the news that Noreen had brutally murdered Maria the day before. Those who found Maria saw that she was covered in blood, her face had been lacerated by savage scratches and the murderer had even gouged out her eyes, claiming that she had been told to do so by certain commands which she couldn't refuse or understand. In a moment of aberration Noreen, whose whole life had been one of kindness and consideration, had changed into a savage murderer. Such a change was beyond human reasoning and defied logic. Immediately I thought of the lady in Christon who told me that the Romans had put a curse on Loxton. Surely one must question why a God-fearing person and one whose previous desires had always been for the good of mankind should, without motive so far as we can discover and quite outside her character, commit so diabolical a crime. We have to ask ourselves whether there was some outside force, some incomprehensible power from another world that not only prompted but compelled the deed. We also have to take into consideration the death of Harry Tiarcks at such a young age, Frank's son being killed in a flying accident and Herman's wife dying in the spring of life . . . and there is more to come.

Noreen O'Connor was found guilty of the murder of Maria Buls and sent to Broadmoor. Later she was paroled and went to live at St Andrew's Hospital in Northampton where she was free to live independently. Before she died on 27 December 1983, she frequently went back to Loxton and Lympsham and visited her old friends whom she had loved and admired some thirty to forty years earlier. Never again did she show any sign of temper, ferociousness or unbecoming behaviour. What was it, we have to ask, that caused that momentary upset in her life?

Let us now go across the valley to Webbington Farm where Herman Tiarcks came to live in 1900. Since those days the M5 motorway has divided Webbington from the major part of Loxton, but in reality it is only a stone's throw away. The Webbington has been a hotel and country club for many years and within its short history it has suffered two major conflagrations, the last one in 1984 causing thousands of pounds' worth of damage. Furthermore, according to some people, the drive into Webbington has also been the scene of psychic phenomena. Many people have seen a ghost dominating the drive on frequent occasions; one farmer I know told me he had driven his tractor right through it. I wonder whether this ghost is another agency the Romans sent to upset the village of Loxton.

Alternatively it could have something to do with Herman Tiarcks himself. In his book *Hunting Reminiscences* he writes, 'When a sportsman dies, he does not go to heaven or hell, he just lives his life over again in someone or something else's body.' Is this, then, his ghost that is seen in the drive? Herman, who was very tall, with legs disproportionate to his body, was so convinced of what he wrote that he continues, 'If ever, when I am gone, a great long-legged fox is found in the neighbourhood, I hope the master or huntsman will give him the benefit of the doubt if he goes to ground.' Undoubtedly Herman was thinking of his own reincarnation.

Add to all the upheaval within the Tiarcks family, the murder of Maria Buls, the ghost of Webbington, the countless motor accidents, the shootings and the conflagrations in the village, one begins to wonder whether that lady in Christon had had a revelation when she spoke about her neighbouring village. I must say, however, that I have not yet met anyone in Loxton who believes in the Roman curse. Every incident I have mentioned, they claim, has a perfectly genuine explanation. I must say I had come to the same point of view until making my way through Loxton some time later, when I decided to call on someone at random.

'Curse?' said the man who had come to the door. 'I don't know, but there is certainly something that goes on that I fail to understand. Take, for instance, my young boy. He was only about two when he first told me that he had seen someone come out of the wall in his bedroom. Both my wife and I took it with a pinch of salt. However, for many nights after he had told us of his fears, my wife and I would take turns to sit by his bed, sometimes up to an hour after we were certain he was fast asleep. Yet, as soon as we left his side he began to cry out for us. It was only after we had begun to suffer from fatigue that we decided to call in the doctor. "A boy of his age, only two, could not possibly imagine such things," said the doctor.

'Later, however, it became my turn either to see things or have a vivid imagination. One night I sat in the drawing-room of my house reading. I remember it was about some lonely little village. I had become so engrossed with the author's easy way of leading me down unknown paths and into unknown places that when I first heard the noise, I considered it all a part of the author's enthralling and enchanting way of capturing his readers. The noise meant nothing to me; it was as if it were something out of my ken.

'However, when it manifested itself a second time I came out of my reverie, put down my book and listened more intently. I had now heard something which had nothing to do with the book I was reading. It was a noise caused by something close at hand . . . it sounded as though a child or children were tiptoeing along the landing or corridor above me. Instinctively, sensing it to be my children, I rose quietly to enable me to come upon them unexpectedly at their pranks, reprehend them and send them back to bed. But on climbing the stairs there was not a child in sight and my children, in different bedrooms, were sleeping soundly. There was no pretence. The children were undoubtedly asleep and dead to the world.

'I went downstairs and once more began reading my book, determined that I would not be intimidated and also resolved that I would not say a thing to my wife. When some fourteen days had gone by without any more disturbance I began to wonder whether the whole thing had been a dream.

'However, on the following Sunday evening, as I sat at home with my wife, I heard a similar noise to the one I had heard on my own. I did nothing. Eventually my wife asked whether I had heard a noise from above. "A noise?" I asked questioningly. "Yes, a noise . . . it is one of the children running along the landing upstairs. I must go up and stop them." I heard my wife go into the childrens' separate rooms. Then she came down, shuddering involuntarily, to tell me there was nothing and the children were sound asleep. And yet, as she sat down in her armchair, there was a shrill of laughter from above. It was not only incredible – it was vexatious. It was as though eyes were looking down on us and we were being teased by unseen spirits, but we could see nothing in return. I was at a loss to know what to do.

'On another occasion, when we were both out for the night leaving a babysitter, a man, alone in the house, we came back to see him striding up and down the room, endeavouring by all means in his power to contain himself. "It's haunted," he said, "this place is haunted. Why didn't you tell me? The place is literally haunted, you should have told me."

'Some weeks after that we called in the local parson, a person answering to my own name, who, with the Bishop's permission, came and exorcised the place.'

The man who told me all this showed me the exact spots where prayers had been said. When I later met his wife, she told me her story without any prompting from her husband, and it was almost word for word what he had told me. This was no fabrication . . . it was real.

4: *The Miraculous*

He Came Back from the Dead. He Rose from his Coffin.

He Came Back from the Dead

On the B3188 Washford – Wiveliscombe road there is a fascinating hamlet by the name of Combe Sydenham. It may be of interest to know that the Combe means valley and the Sydenham refers to the lord of the manor, as in the case of similar

Combe Sydenham, the home of Sir George Sydenham

names such as Combe Martin in Devon and many, many more. Combe Sydenham was therefore the home of Sir George Sydenham over whose main door we read: 'This door of George's is open except to ungrateful souls'. I mention Sir George Sydenham because he is one of the many Sydenhams in Somerset. There is a memorial to Sir George in Stogumber Church. There is a memorial to a Sydenham in Dulverton Church and Sydenhams are also referred to in the manor and the delightful little church at Brympton D'Evercy. To which Sydenham we owe the prophecy that he would return to life after death is hard to surmise. We do know, however, he was a Major George Sydenham.

Before we enter upon this story one has to admit that there have been thousands of people who have testified to their having seen a ghost. At the same time there are also thousands who are not so easily convinced that ghosts exist at all and consider all sightings as figments of the imagination. Samuel Johnson once wrote that the world had been in existence for a long time, but 'still it is undecided whether or not there has ever been an instance of the spirit of any person appearing after death. All argument is against it; but all belief is for it.'

We have all heard of Marley's ghost in Dicken's *Christmas Carol*. Pope occasionally mentions ghosts in his writings, while Shakespeare quotes them frequently. The people who deny their existence base their premise on the fact that they themselves have never seen one. But, as Joseph Granvill, a Doctor of Divinity and a Fellow of the Royal Society, says:

> Matters of fact well proved ought not to be denied because we cannot conceive how they can be performed. Nor is it a reasonable method of inference to presume the thing impossible, and thence to conclude that the fact cannot be proved.

In his book, *The Most Haunted House in England*, Harry Price, the author, tells us how he invited hundreds of witnesses, some of whom were people of great eminence, to attest the paranormal happenings of Borley Rectory in Suffolk before it was destroyed by fire in 1939. The vast majority of people who went to Borley had to admit to happenings which they could only conclude were incomprehensible. Indeed, it is a fact that after much investigation of psychic phenomena at Borley, a skeleton of a lady, believed to be a murdered nun, was unearthed beneath the floor of the rectory. Was this the cause of all the paranormal happenings that were testified to by some of the most noted men in this country at the time?

We have not the time to make such investigations, neither is it the nature of this book to do so, but for our interest let me quote from the book, *The Most Haunted House in England*, the story of one invited witness.

Fred Cartwright, a journeyman carpenter who lived near Borley in Suffolk, used to pass Borley Rectory every morning on his way to work. He generally started his journey, coming from the direction of Sudbury, just as it was beginning to get light. In the autumn of 1927 he began to see things which astounded him, and at a time when no one was occupying the rectory. His story is related as follows:

> On the second day he saw a Sister of Mercy (or nun) standing outside the rectory by the first drive gate. She looked normal and did not speak, and Cartwright went on his way. He wondered what she was waiting for. This was on a Tuesday. On the following Friday morning, at the same time and place, he saw her again. She seemed tired, and her eyes were closed. But he still thought she was human. The third time he saw her, at the same hour and place, was on the following Wednesday. She again had her eyes closed as in sleep, and as he passed he noticed that she seemed tired and ill. He thought he would ask her whether she needed assistance. He suddenly turned to do so, but she had vanished. She made no sound, and he concluded that she had noiselessly entered

> the rectory, which was unoccupied, although he did not know it. The last time he saw the nun was on the following Friday morning, and she was still standing by the drive gate. As he approached he decided to say 'Good Morning' to her, but before he had reached the gate she had gone. He did not actually see her vanish, but one moment she was there, the next she was not. Thoroughly puzzled, he opened the gate with difficulty – and explored the drive and grounds. There was no sign of her. It was not until he related the incident to his friends at Sudbury subsequently that he learned the story of the rectory.

Harry Price was described by the *Times Literary Supplement* on 26 December 1942, as having done more 'than anyone of this generation to establish psychical research on a scientific basis'.

But to return to Major George Sydenham. In 1680 the major had a very great friend by the name of Captain Dyke. They often discussed, so it is said, the theology of the day and the theory of the resurrection of the dead. Apparently Major George believed in an afterlife, to which belief the Captain could not subscribe. Although they agreed to differ, they did decide on one thing: that whoever died first he would try and come back from the grave and appear to the other as proof of an afterlife. Major George Sydenham was the first to die, and three weeks later he appeared to the captain in his bedroom in the light of the day.

Now, the Revd John Flavell, a Doctor of Divinity who subsequently lectured all over the county and elsewhere on Major George Sydenham's reappearance, had some very startling things to say about this gentleman's return to earth. First of all he said:

> The captain was so taken aback by the reappearance of Major George that he came down to breakfast in the morning

> with his eyes staring and his whole body shaking and trembling. He declared before an astounded and startled company, 'I have seen the Major. If ever I saw him in my life, I have seen him this morning, and it was also after it was light.'

The Revd Flavell may have convinced many people of the truth of his story but he did not convince everyone. There were still many who had grave suspicions. They argued it was a mere hallucination on the captain's part due to the fact that he was getting old and senile and was therefore not to be relied upon. And so the arguments have continued down the ages.

Even as late as 1921 the major's reappearance was still being discussed. That year an article relating to 'Sydenham's Ghost' was featured in a west Somerset newspaper which included some rather sceptical and critical remarks to which Dr George F. Sydenham, a descendent of Major George, took exception. In replying to this article he wrote in the same west Somerset newspaper the following letter:

> Sir, It is not a matter of public interest to relate what I have seen and what has been related to me by others worthy of credence. But the appearance of Major George Sydenham is a matter of history, and therefore is of public interest.

He Rose from his Coffin

I suppose the most beautiful part of Frome, a town bordering on Wiltshire, is a place called Vallis. It is a wonderful valley or glen, north-west of the town itself, where the woods close in at the very edge of the Mendip Hills.

In the time of King Henry IV (1399–1413) the Manor of Vallis was granted by the king to John Payne of London, whose daughter and heiress married Edmund Leversege, and the manor remained in the Leverseges' hands until Sir Thomas Thynne bought it in the reign of King James I (1625–44).

Soon after Edmund Leversege had married and inherited the family estates, however, he began to meddle in the black art of magic, an exercise liberally practised in the fourteenth and fifteenth centuries. He also lived a wild life of dissipation, until one day he was struck down and died during one of his orgies. This incident very soon became the talk of the town and most people argued that so vile a wretch as Edmund Leversege, as he had proved himself to be, should never be buried in a sacred building. They undoubtedly knew that over the centuries all the Leverseges had been buried in the parish church of Frome, in their own private vault.

Vicious arguments arose on both sides as to how the matter should be resolved and, as it appeared the feud would never be healed, it was finally decided by the relatives to take the body, in secrecy, to the vault in the church in the dead of night. One has to say this was not an unusual practice in those days. From the manor-house in Vallis, under cover of darkness, the mourners and pallbearers walked along the undulating private way through the fields on the estate to the main road that led to the church. It was a quiet, dignified procession of people who made their way to the church on that woe-begotten night. They did not wish to see anybody and they did not wish to be seen, knowing that the news would spread like wildfire.

Having reached the gate leading to the estate, they proceeded slowly uphill towards the parish church in the centre of the town. Luckily, everywhere was quiet. Apparently the inhabitants of Frome were asleep in their beds as not a light was seen in any of the houses. Up to that moment they were fortunate for although they had anticipated hostility from the townspeople, they had not encountered a single soul. They had crossed over the rugged fields, passed into the country and walked through the built-up areas of the town approaching the church without being seen.

The funeral procession now passed down the very narrow entrance that led to the church, and was approaching the door. All had gone according to plan and they were indeed very thankful . . .

But 'fore they reached the dim lit church
  A knock the bearers heard;
At first so faint, it sounded like
  The pecking of a bird;
They stopped and asked, now all afraid,
By whom it was the noise was made.

Then for a time the tapping ceased
  Till it was heard once more;
It sounded now, the mourners said,
  More urgent than before:
And every face in that small crowd
Was whiter than the burial shroud.

The sound came not from far away,
  But nearer, close at hand,
As though the devil hovering there
  Had issued a command
To knock and knock so they who'd hear
Would soon be paralysed with fear.

The bearers now were terrified,
  For they could not deny
The sound came from the coffin which
  They now bore shoulder high:
And each man asked the one ahead
Could sounds like that come from the dead?

They dropped the coffin in their fright;
  Then one by one the screws
Were loosened by the family, who
  Had no will to refuse;
With plaintive cry and steadfast bid
They scrambled to remove the lid.

But 'fore the lid was taken off
  And fearful men had fled,
A yell came from the one inside
  Whom mourners knew was dead,
A yell that curdled flesh and blood
Through all that close knit neighbourhood.

They tore aside the lid and shroud
  In ever quickening drive
Till Edmund Leversege sat up
  Now breathing and alive.
Yes, in search of truth – it must be said,
He was alive – who once was dead.

When Edmund Leversege eventually died, an emaciated effigy of him in the shape of a skeleton, was placed under the stone slab of his tomb in the Lady Chapel of the parish church of Frome. This was a witness to all that it is better by far to be on the side of God, than on the side of the devil.

5: *Witches*

Sally in the Woods. The Charming Witch of Withycombe. Witches of a Different Breed.

SALLY IN THE WOODS

If ever you find yourself Batheaston way, near Bath, you must take the opportunity of going along the A363 Bradford-on-Avon road. Within 2 miles of Bathford you will see a wood stretching for some 1 to 3 miles along the hillside, on the summit of which there is a tower.

This folly was built many years ago by Wade Brown, lord of Monkton Farleigh Manor, undoubtedly to satisfy a whim of his, but more particularly to give work to the poor and unemployed during a period of great recession. There is nothing sinister about that noble edifice that crowns the hill, but the same cannot be said of the region below which, to the passer-by, is merely a beautiful area of trees stretching, as I have already remarked, along the hillside. But let us enter into the woods and see what they have in store for us. This area of trees is known as 'Sally in the Woods', referring, so we are told, to a lady who lived in a cottage all on her own for many, many years. It is said she was the widow of a gamekeeper by the name of Gibson who worked on the estate of the Skrine family, lords of the manor of Warleigh. To other people, however, she was far more than that.

For years it was known that these lonely woods were not only riddled with caverns and caves, but were also the haunt of hermits and the outcasts of society. Sally, living in her cottage, however deteriorated it may have become, stood in such a class of her own that these people resorted to her for advice and care. She was the knowledgeable one, the recluse, the untouchable – in fact, some considered her no less than a witch with remarkable powers. In truth it is said that when she died at a fabulous age, the lord of the manor of Warleigh had his carpenter set fire to the cottage and that, as the cottage burned, out of the centre of it came a sepulchral cry that made the carpenter run for his life. He had never heard anything like it before, he said, and even after many years that cry was still ringing in his ears.

It is maintained, and I cannot vouch for the truth of this although it is well authenticated, that the carpenter said that as the sepulchral cry rang out through the woods, something flew out of the chimney as the cottage became engulfed with flames . . . and that something . . . looked uncommonly like a witch.

I must leave it entirely to you whether you believe that or not, but it is significant, is it not, that even today that lonely place on the hillside is known as 'Sally in the Woods'. Have you ever heard of another wood or forest or copse given a name like that? I do not believe you have – which not only makes the wood unique, but Sally, a very redoubtable character indeed.

The Charming Witch of Withycombe

Within two miles of Minehead, just off the main road, there is a small village by the name of Withycombe. For those who do not know Somerset very well, I have to stress, not Withypool,

Sandell Manor, built in 1588 and now known as Sandhill Farm, was once the home of the charming witch of Withycombe

nor Widdicombe – this village is Withycombe. Here we find a church on our right, with small cottages lining the other side of this attractive, hilly village. If we continue through the village we find an unbridged ford on our left and, should we cross it and ascend the hill beyond, we would go down the other side and see a rather dull Elizabethan manor, built in 1588, the year of the Armada. It is now known as Sandhill Farm but, at the beginning of the seventeenth century, it was known as Sandell Manor. This was once the home of Joan Carne. If we go into the twelfth-century church, passing recumbent effigies on our left and right, we pass through the chancel screen. On the north wall of the chancel is a memorial tablet in memory of Joan Carne of Sandell, which reads thus:

> Here lyeth ye Bodie of Joan Carne of Sandell who was
> thrice married, first unto John Newton of Sandell, Gent.
> Afterward unto Charles Windham, Esq and last of all

> unto Thomas Carne of Eweney in Y Countie of Glenerga, Esquire. She dyed on Y nyne and Twentieth Daye of October in the Yeare of our Lord 1612.

According to all that I have heard, Joan Carne was a very charming lady; so beautiful that every young man in the vicinity was captivated by her. It was her charms that brought John Newton to her side. Within weeks he had married her, and thus she became one of the most affluent ladies in the place. But John soon died. He was hardly forgotten before Charles Windham came to offer his hand, and very soon Joan was leading him down the aisle of the village church. Now when he died soon after marriage, making Joan richer than ever, tongues began to wag in the village. And one has to remember that this was the beginning of the seventeenth century, when witches were abroad in the land. Consequently, Joan Carne was very soon being spoken of as the charming witch of Withycombe. But that did not keep away Thomas Carne. He had heard of this charming lady from as far away as Eweney in the county of Glenerga (Glamorgan) and once more a bridal march was being played in the twelfth-century church of St Nicholas.

Need anything more be said? Very soon after the wedding Thomas Carne was taken seriously ill. His relatives, having heard what the local people were saying, came to protect Thomas from his wife. Be that as it may, Thomas Carne died. And Joan, within a few years, had become the richest lady, not only in the county, but far and wide. Finally, on 29 October 1612, Joan Carne herself passed away, and now there was money to spare for someone . . . and the vultures came to pick their prize.

The relatives saw to it that Joan Carne, after the service in the church at Withycombe, was well and truly laid, as indeed all witches and suicides were in those days. They had her coffin barred to the ground and saw the grave filled. And then, with as much decorum as possible, but with singing in their hearts, they got into their vehicles and sang all the way home to Sandell Manor to hear the will read. But as they opened the front door of the glorious old Elizabethan manor, who should they see but Joan Carne, standing before them with all her usual charm, frying eggs and bacon in a pan.

Here was a climax indeed. Some of the relatives immediately rushed over to Watchet to fetch the parish priest (why the local parish priest would not do, I do not know) who, on their orders, exorcised the manor and drove the charming witch of Withycombe, or her ghost, into the pond. But I can assure you that that is not the end of the story.

There is a belief in Somerset that the strong personalities whose ghosts have been exorcised, such as, for instance, the hanging judge, Sir John Popham of Wellington and Madam Joan Carne, *can* and *do* return by one cockstride each year. I can furthermore assure you that when anything goes wrong Withycombe way, people say that Madam Joan Carne is at it again.

Witches of a Different Breed

There is no doubt that the majority of people today repudiate such stories as 'Sally in the Woods' or the 'Charming Witch of Withycombe', and I suppose such an attitude is understandable. I think we may be forgiven for rejecting such stories of witches flying through the air on broom sticks. Such an outlook, we can say, would not stand up to intellectual debate. Yet we have to remember that Shakespeare and numerous Elizabethan writers refer to witches doing rather remarkable things. But whatever we think, there is no doubt that witches did exist in the fifteenth and sixteenth centuries as we will see from the history below. I think it is also probable that witches moved from place to place.

Perched on the side of a hill in Winscombe, near Weston-super-Mare, is a charming fifteenth-century church boasting a Norman font. If one looks closely at the font one will see that there are iron fixtures embedded in the stonework which implies that the lid of the font was once locked, undoubtedly to prevent holy water being stolen, chiefly, it has been suggested, by witches. There is also a Norman font in the church of Chelwood on the A368 Churchill–Bath road with similar wrought iron attachments. There must have been some reason to cause the church authorities to lock the lids on to the font so securely in days gone by.

We have also to include in our list of witches the place known as Wookey Hole near Cheddar. Whatever the cynic may say, the Witch of Wookey is in no way a modern phenomenon nor a modern advertising ruse. She or her shape was first mentioned as far back as 1470 when William of Worcester (Falstaff's secretary) visited the caves. But to enable us to go more thoroughly into this matter of witches, let me take you to Wincanton, a town in Somerset, on the border of Dorset.

In 1664 a lady of Wincanton, called Elizabeth Style, confessed to being in touch with the devil, if I am to believe what I have read in *Sadducismus Triumphatus*, and since I do not wish personally to convince you by debate alone, I give you here a précis of her own confession:

> About ten years ago the devil appeared to me in the garb of a handsome man, and afterward in the shape of a black dog. He promised me money and a long life, on the conditions of signing a bond with my blood and handing my soul over to him and permitting him to suck my blood when he desired it. This I granted him after four solicitations, upon which he pricked the fourth finger of my right hand between the middle and the upper joint. For this favour the devil gave me sixpence and vanished with the paper. And ever after he often appeared to me in the shape

> of a man, dog, cat or fly. And when I desired to harm anyone, I called the spirit of the name of Robin and invoked him in the following manner: 'O Satan give me my purpose.' About a month before this trial I desired to harm Elizabeth Hall and to thrust thorns into her flesh, so accordingly a meeting was held on the common near Trister Gate, where I met Alice Duke, Ann Bishop, and Mary Penny; Alice Duke having brought a picture in wax, which was intended for Elizabeth Hall, to be baptised by Satan, who appearing in black clothes performed the ceremony by anointing the effigy with oil and saying: 'I baptise thee with oil. . . .'
>
> Then the figure in wax was struck through with thorns by all present. After which they had wine, cakes, and roast meat provided by the gentleman in black. When I wished to injure man or beast I made an image of the person or the beast in wax, which must be baptised by the devil, for even our power is limited by the will of the master. The belief of the country people in witches and wizards possessing the power of overlooking is not yet extinct.

May I presume to explain that the approved method of injuring or killing one's enemy was to make an image of him or her in wax, and then stick thorns or pins into it accompanied by various diabolical ceremonies.

In order to confirm the truth of this confession let us travel north and take an unclassified road in an easterly direction towards Brewham. Here, in the seventeenth century, lived Margaret Agar. She said that if she wished to do harm to her adversaries:

> she sticks a thorn towards the heart of a picture of her adversary which has been made in black wax, saying, 'a plague on you'. This is what she did to hurt Elizabeth Cornish who, she admitted, had been ill ever since. She also

> stuck a thorn into the heart of a figure representing John Talbot of Brewham, which caused his death.

I suppose one may be forgiven for believing all this to be the silly superstition of an obscure Somerset village of a past age for surely such statements could not stand up to a healthy and educated debate today. It was, one is tempted to say, no more than village superstition and certainly could not have been believed by an educated people. Well, let us see whether this is so. For a moment, let us leave these obscure little villages in the county of Somerset and even the country itself, and cross the channel to France. Let us take ourselves to what was then considered to be the very centre of the civilized world, and learn how the courtiers of King Louis XIV avenged themselves of their enemies. This is what they did, and I now quote:

> If you wish to kill your enemy, make a wax figure of him, concentrate all the intensity of your hatred upon it, take a needle and give a blow straight at the heart, and his death will be instantaneous.

At a trial in Paris in 1619 one of the pieces of evidence was a sheep's heart stuck full of nails and very long pins.

Surely that is sufficient evidence to prove that this part of Somerset was certainly not out of touch with the civilized world, nor its beliefs mere superstition, as one from outside may have first believed.

6: *Hangings*

John Walford's Gibbet. Jack White's Gibbet, Heddon Oak.

JOHN WALFORD'S GIBBET

Near the second turning on the left, immediately after passing Nether Stowey on the A39 to Minehead, there is a signpost pointing in the direction of the Quantock Hills and a superb Somerset village by the name of Crowcombe. After negotiating a broad sweep to the left and driving about half a mile there is a sharp turning to the right where one should stop. An Ordnance Survey map will suggest that this spot is called Walford's Gibbet.

John Walford, a tall, handsome, tender-hearted and prepossessing young man, was born at Over Stowey in the year 1765. By trade he was a charcoal-burner. He fell in love with Ann Rice (or Rich), a lovely, well educated, miller's daughter who lived in the same village. When eventually the banns of marriage were called in Over Stowey Church, John Walford's selfish and possessive step-mother stood up and opposed the marriage. This was a bitter disappointment to both John and Ann for, in those days, if banns of marriage were opposed, one could say the wedding was off . . . and John and Ann were deeply in love. Although they still continued to meet, albeit infrequently, evil tongues, led by John's step-mother, eventually forced them to separate.

But as John Walford tended the charcoal burning in his lonely hut over the Quantock Hills, he was noticed by a conspiring, though slovenly and stupid girl by the name of Jane Thorney. Although stupid, she possessed a natural craftiness and began to visit him night after night, with the perhaps unsurprising result that she became pregnant. Now in those days, if a couple found themselves in this predicament, they got married and, on 18 June 1789, John (now twenty-four) married her. And although he was not in love with her, he meant to keep his bond for did I not say that he was a loyal and tender-hearted young man. However, on 4 July (only seventeen days after the marriage) they were walking to the Castle of Comfort, an inn on the main A39 road, when they quarrelled and, in that moment, John remembered his first love, Ann. In a flash of temper he struck Jane to the ground – DEAD.

He was tried at Bridgwater Assize on 18 August 1789 by Lord Kenyon. The trial lasted not three weeks, as they may do today, but three hours, and John was found guilty of wilful murder, although the only evidence was of a circumstantial nature. Recognizing that the accused who stood before him was a young man of sterling character, it is said that the judge broke down in tears as he ordered John to be hanged and his body to be delivered to the surgeons to be anatomized. Despite this the jury petitioned that, as there had been three murders in that village within living memory, he should be hanged on a gibbet, near the spot where the crime was committed, and left to hang.

On the day of the hanging he was put in a cart, had his last drink in the George at Nether Stowey, and was then taken to Bincombe, overlooking Doddington village, to the corner on the Quantock Hills where the gibbet had been placed. As John Walford stood in the cart, beneath the gibbet, he asked whether he might be allowed to see his old love, Ann, and she, who had been crouching round the corner, was brought to him on the cart. It is said that so lovingly the couple spoke one to the other, that they who had come especially to stand and stare and almost certainly to throw disparaging remarks, very soon repented and instead gave themselves to silence and to prayer. There was no bitterness, no slinging of insults or such denigration as predominated most 'Hang Fair' days in Ilchester or wherever a gibbet was raised on a convenient site for all to see. The crowds that had assembled for sport were so taken aback by John's obvious sincerity and love for Ann that they were transfixed to the spot and powerless to assist. In fact, slowly but surely, those who had come to mock John as he stood beneath the gibbet, were unconsciously being swayed to come out on his side especially when, at the very moment John was about to give Ann his last kiss on earth, the guards intervened by snatching her, struggling, from his reaches so that the kiss fell to the ground wasted. Furthermore, when the crowd saw, as a result, tears welling from John's eyes and running down those handsome features, it so stunned the dazed onlookers that men who had never prayed for years or had never prayed in their lives joined with the chaplain in saying 'Amen' as the soul of John Walford was carried into eternity. Never, never had hundreds of people been so universally moved. It was as though, they said, they could see John's soul being borne by angels upwards until all disappeared into the heavens above.

In those days, it must be remembered, that hangings were mostly public affairs. A 'Hang Fair' day was an occasion at which thousands of people gathered, but most of the individuals hanged on gibbets throughout the county have been forgotten with the passage of time. Very few are remembered. In Walford's case people who had come from near and far to witness the scene were so captivated by all they saw that Somerset people still talk of Walford's Gibbet with the deepest respect. They who were present, and could express themselves, declared that nothing could have been so poignant. If a needle had dropped to the ground that day, they said, it would have been heard by the 3,000 people who stood on the side of the glorious Quantocks to watch the hanging of John Walford. They swore that foxes ceased to yelp, rooks to caw, the wind to blow and even the birds resisted singing for a few moments. On that afternoon, on the Quantock Hills, when John Walford was launched into eternity, there was not a man, even the roughest of the rough, who had not a tear in his eye.

The irony of this case is that the gibbet stood directly facing the front door of Walford's step-mother's home, a mere quarter of a mile away, and she could not go outside her home without seeing John's remains swinging in the air. His body was left hanging for one whole year before the remains, a few bones, were buried on the spot. But the gibbet remained until the beginning of this century. It had stood on that one spot for one hundred years and that is why, should you read an Ordnance Survey map, you would see, in bold capitals, this corner designated as John Walford's Gibbet.

If you had read the *Bath and Bristol Magazine* for the year 1797 you would have read the epilogue to the story that I have just told you. Here is what it said:

> After hanging the usual time the body was taken down, placed in an iron cage and then suspended on the gibbet, and it was a common saying that Walford looked better hanged than most men look alive.

Jack White's Gibbet

Although at the beginning of the eighteenth century wages and living standards were low in Wincanton, yet it is a remarkable fact that the inns in the town were always well patronized. Robert Sutton, a messenger with whom everyone consorted for news, always knew where he could find a willing audience. As he was wining and dining at the Sun Inn a large number of men had gathered round. He was telling his eager listeners stories of the latest execution at Tyburn; an attack on the mail coach; the latest sentence meted out at the assizes and, on the occasion of which I am speaking, one of his most eager listeners was a person by the name of Jack White.

Jack White was born in Wincanton, and baptized on 16 December 1690. So far as we know, his parents, Nicholas and Elizabeth, had given him a Christian education and a good upbringing. On 19 May 1716, Jack White married Sarah Slade at the parish church and for a long period he seemed to have lived an honest life. Subsequently, one has to admit, there were certain accusations made against him, including killing his only child, but these were never proven. In the days when a police force such as we have today was unknown, one could get away with many things, including murder, but even so, Jack White's character appears at that time to have been blameless.

Jack, who had become fascinated by the messenger Robert Sutton, was still eagerly listening to him telling him stories of far and wide, of adventure and misadventure, when most of the other customers had left, and during Sutton's peroration the two men drank deeper and deeper. In due course the messenger, who had only a little knowledge of the topography of Wincanton and its environs, asked Jack whether he would give him directions to certain villages and hamlets where he had to deliver mail. Jack told him he was not only pleased to do so but would willingly accompany him to any place he desired if it would ease the situation for him. Robert Sutton was so pleased with Jack's friendliness that he involuntarily warmed towards him.

Before the two men had gone very far they met two women and Jack, still under the influence of drink, became playful and kissed one of them. But when he tried his advances on the other woman he met with such stiff opposition that he tried to throw her to the ground. Robert Sutton took the woman's part, and from that moment Jack's attitude towards him changed. When the ladies had gone, Sutton, under the influence of drink, laid down to go to sleep and while he was asleep Jack White stealthily took a stake from the hedge, crashed Sutton across the head, knocked out one of his eyes, and ran the stake into his mouth and so through his neck. He either could not or dare not touch the body to hide it and consequently it was soon found. Within days the whole country rang with the news of the savage murder and within weeks Jack was apprehended and accused. Although many stories have been told about the manner in which he was apprehended, it is extremely difficult to be certain of the facts.

One version of the story suggests that the body of Robert Sutton was laid out in the church porch, with the clergy and magistrates standing beside it. All the people in the neighbourhood came in crowds to witness the scene. To refuse to come would have given cause for suspicion and would be even tantamount to guilt. The men passed in procession up the churchyard path and each lifted his hat and laid his hand upon the corpse since it was believed that, when the murderer touched it, blood would flow from the poor victim's wounds. When Jack White's turn came to touch the body a kind of shuddering gasp of expectation ran through the crowd. 'He has not touched him; he has not touched him,' someone cried. And at that word the unhappy man withdrew his hand trembling from head to foot. His guilt had been proven.

It is hard to separate truth from fiction but of one fact we are certain, and that is that a murder was committed, and in such a diabolical manner that many legends have grown around the actual occurrence of his being apprehended. Facts are facts, fiction is fiction and the facts of Jack White's case are that when he was safe in Ilchester gaol, all he could say was that the hounds of hell had pursued him to commit the fatal deed. He was sentenced to death by Mr Baron Thompson at the Bridgwater Assize on 6 August 1730, and was condemned to be hanged.

On Wednesday 19 August, two weeks after the sentence and after the condemned man had made a full confession, he was hanged at the crossroads near where the murder was committed where the road from Bratton Seymour to Holton crosses the A371 from Wincanton to Castle Cary. It is marked on an Ordnance Survey map as Jack White's Gibbet. Although the A371 is a busy road the crossroads, with a bungalow at one corner and a telephone kiosk at the other, present an exceptionally lonely and eerie atmosphere even today. Opposite the kiosk, backed by a forest of trees, there is a small knoll on which the gibbet once stood and upon which Jack's body was left hanging for many weeks, as a deterrent to all would-be murderers.

Some considerable time after the execution, so it is said, Squire Woodford of Castle Cary had occasion to pass the gibbet late one night after wining and dining in Wincanton. He declared he was not afraid of the darkness or of ghosts and phantoms. Why, he would talk to the corpse of Jack White as he passed by, he said. And he kept his promise. As he passed the crossroads, he said, 'Well Jack, how be ye?' To his horror he heard the corpse reply, 'Jack's cold . . . turble cold.' It is said that the squire never passed that way again after wining and dining in Wincanton!

In Ilchester gaol Jack White confessed to the crime as I have already indicated, and the following is his confession:

> I desire all good Christians to take warning this day by my untimely end. I was born in Wincanton of honest and industrious parents and lived honestly and soberly until the 26th year of my age when I married into an honest family: lived lovingly with my wife: nor was I ever maliciously inclined to hurt man, woman or child until the time when this unfortunate accident happened which that day I little thought of. But

going along Wincanton, one Gilbert at the sign of the Sun called me into his house where I drank hard. When the deceased came in who was in liquor and offered me drink to go along with him, which I agreed to, and went with him out of town, directing him in his way as well as I was able, but being overcome with liquor I laid down to sleep while the deceased went forward, who, missing his way came back to me again and woke me and begged of me to go a little farther with him. I agreed, and in our way met two women, one of whom I saluted, and the other being stubborn, provoked me to strike her, and as far as my memory can retain, the deceased and I had words about them, and also would force me to go along with him to his journey's end, taking a counter out of his pocket, cursing and swearing that it was half a guinea and that he would spend it all upon me. We went on until we came to that fatal place, where through drunkenness and the devil's suggestion I entrenched my hands in his innocent blood for which I beg heartily the forgiveness of God. I die in peace with all mankind, imploring the prayers of all good Christians and commend my soul to the mercy of Jesus Christ on whom I wholly rely for salvation, and whereas several reports have been spread abroad as that I have attempted to poison myself in prison, and that I was accessory to the death of my own child and guilty of robbery, shoplifting and house-breaking, and that I have impeached seventeen or eighteen of my accomplices all which reports I declare before God, as I am a dying man, are false and groundless. I beg the world not to cast any reflections on my relations on account of my shameful end and particularly on my dear and innocent wife, who has behaved herself with real tenderness to me even in a common gaol, and in all respects been a loving wife and a good Christian.

Jack White.

HEDDON OAK

Near Crowcombe, on the A358 Williton–Taunton road, there is a road to the right indicating Stogumber. Within a mile, if we take this road, there are crossroads with Loundesford Lane to the right and Vexford to the left. We should go beyond the crossroads and park our car in a convenient place to allow us to look round and get our bearings. I warn you, however, only do this in the daytime. Whatever you do, refrain from stopping at this point when darkness has pervaded the land. Let me tell you the reason.

At this point there once stood a quaint old oak tree, known as Heddon Oak, with a lateral, gnarled branch stretching over the road. The top part of the tree, undoubtedly due to its dangerous position and its decaying condition, was sawn off in 1980. But the spot remains and is still indicated in the Automobile Association's *Illustrated Road Book* under the heading 'Crowcombe'. Let us now go back into history for a moment.

Some months after the Battle of Sedgemoor on 6 July 1685, which was the last battle fought on English soil, Lord Chief Justice Jeffreys, the 'Bloody Judge', set out on the western Assizes to deal with those who had fought on the side of the Duke of Monmouth in opposition to King James II. The judge had been ordered by the king (who had vanquished the Duke of Monmouth) to make an example of those rebels from the west country; in particular, those of Somerset. This was undoubtedly due to the fact that the battle had been fought in that county. Assizes were held at Winchester, Salisbury, Dorchester, Exeter, Taunton and Wells, where the rank and file of the rebels were dealt with very harshly. About 300 were executed in numerous villages in Somerset alone, and their bodies were drawn and quartered and hung at crossroads and vantage points all over the county. Another 849 of those who were

Judge Jeffreys, the 'Bloody Judge' of Somerset

inveigled into fighting on the side of Monmouth were transported to Barbados while hundreds of others were whipped through the streets.

It is difficult for us today to fully appreciate the cruelty and bestiality of these proceedings. Deliberate cruel measures were handed out by the 'Bloody Judge' to at least thirty-four towns and villages in Somerset. The number of those whom Judge Jeffreys assigned to be hanged, drawn and quartered and the places in Somerset where these hangings took place are as follows: Axbridge 6; Bridgwater 9; Bruton 3; Castle Cary 3; Chard 12; Chewton Mendip 2; Cothelstone 2; Crewkerne 10; Dulverton 3; Dunster 3; Frome 12; Glastonbury 5; Ilchester 12; Ilminster 12; Langport 3; Milborne Port 2; Minehead 6; Nether Stowey 3; Norton St Philip 13; Porlock 2; Shepton Mallet 12; Somerton 7; Stogursey 2; Taunton 19; Wellington 3; Wells 8; Wincanton 7; Wiveliscombe 3; Wrington 3; and Yeovil 7.

One other place in Somerset where these bestial hangings took place was at Heddon Oak, Stogumber. Three rebels were hanged here: George Gillard, John Lockstone and Arthur Williams. It is said by some that sometimes the chains on which they were hanged can still be heard rattling at night even today. I cannot vouch for the truth of that.

However, when I first directed your attention to Heddon Oak I requested you not to stay on this spot at night, for I did not wish you to have anything like my own experience. When first I travelled this way I knew nothing of Heddon Oak or of the three men being hanged from it in the seventeenth century. I was only on this spot because my car had stalled, and I could not get it to start. While I waited for someone to help me . . .

I stood at the crossroads in the dead of the night
On my way to Stogumber, for my car wouldn't go;
In the cold blustery wind there was no one in sight
As I looked for my torch, my position to know.

In a way I was lucky, for I soon found a farm,
Where I hastily phoned to 'the best man by far',
Who said he would hurry, and I'd come to no harm
If I put on my lights indicating my car.

I returned to the crossroads and shut myself in,
As the wind tore at branches grown hard by the cold,
Yet an uneasy silence bore down o'er the scene,
And I felt myself growing less consciously bold.

I could hardly have stopped at a more eerie place;
Apprehensions increased by alarming degrees,
And I heard timid cries as I came face to face
With silhouetted men hanging down from the trees.

It was hard to conceive that there were things so weird,
So I plucked up my courage, and went closer to see;
The cries kept on calling, but the men disappeared,
Yet back in my car they were beckoning me.

As the rain touched my car screen it turned into ice;
While the figures before me danced in the car light;
My head was now singing as though held in a vice
While the faces of skulls seemed to laugh at my plight.

It was such a relief when my helper arrived,
Who amazed me by starting my car at a stroke;
He listened as I told him I'd hardly survived,
'Well, you see,' he said, pointing, 'That IS Heddon Oak.'

Since then I have read of the Bloody Assize
And of Judge Jeffreys hanging some three hundred men;
And I think I'm now sure why this place horrifies
While similar places are not thought of again.

Like Taunton or Bruton, where like vengeance was wrought,
Or at Axbridge and Wells and near Glastonbury Tor,
Or like Frome and Ilchester and charming Langport,
Or like Dunster and Chard, some three dozen or more.

I have gone back in daylight to see Heddon Oak,
With its lateral branches as though made to a mould,
Still wonderfully strong as when Jeffreys first spoke,
Still looking like gallows, though four hundred years old.

But I've never gone back in the dark or moonlight;
A team of black horses would only drag me in vain;
For the things that I saw on that ill-fated night
I'll do all in power to avoid seeing again.

7: Graves at the Crossroads

Cannard's Grave. Mary's Grave. Molly Hunt.

CANNARD'S GRAVE

Within a mile of Shepton Mallet the A37 Bath–Bristol/ Weymouth road will take us through a rather characterless village known as Cannard's Grave. On the right hand side of this village is a tall, thin, gaunt, macabre-looking building known as Cannard's Grave Inn, about which many wonderful stories have been woven. For centuries this inn had been the only meeting-place for stage-coach travellers for many, many miles and was therefore well known to those who travelled regularly from place to place. Obversely, it was not so well known to those who travelled very infrequently.

Should you approach Cannard's Grave Inn in the evening, when darkness is beginning to descend over the land, I am convinced that, should you give yourself time to absorb the atmosphere, you would soon begin to experience a deep sense of the paranormal, even though today there is a constant flow of traffic to divert our thoughts. The clouds seem to rush overhead as though frightened to stay too long in this spot, and although it may be calm elsewhere, the wind always seems to blow, and blow colder here. Even the inn begins to take on a ghostly aspect on this corner site and one experiences a feeling of intense loneliness and, indeed, desolation.

When last I called at Cannard's Grave Inn the landlord told me that if one stood on the roof, it was plain to see that the building itself had been erected, either intentionally or otherwise, in the shape of a coffin. He also told me that he and his wife and guests had often heard movements in the place which defied logical explanation. Now, if you wonder why this place produces such an atmosphere, filling locals and strangers alike with dreadful forebodings, you will have to go back into history to find the answer.

It is said that in the early seventeenth century Giles Cannard, a kindly dispositioned soul, was landlord of the stage-coach inn. Eventually, however, he found that drugging his overnight guests and stealing from them when they were in a drugged or drunken stupor was a far easier and quicker way of amassing a fortune than by selling beer or a bed for the night. So easy did this work become that, before long, Giles, who had also taken to the bottle, began to find it difficult to distinguish between right and wrong. The cosy, warm, stage-coach inn, on that very lonely road, soon became a place of debauchery, corruption and crime, and some have even suggested murder. Kate, Gile's wife, who was very devoted to him, realizing the depths to which he had fallen, constantly endeavoured to make him change his way of life. On each occasion her pleadings met with some success until another client was seen as easy picking. Seeing that her pleadings were of no avail, the constant frustration and worry eventually made her ill, drove her to despair and, finally, to her bed.

It may seem strange to many people that, since all these events took place in the early seventeenth century, I am so intimate with the history of Cannard's Grave Inn and the Cannard family itself. But it is not as strange as it may seem for the story has been written over and over again, although the accounts differ one from the other. However, I have to admit the one advantage I do have is that a gentleman, having the same interests as myself, once told me of his own personal experience concerning the landlord of Cannard's Grave Inn.

Some time ago, he told me, he had been travelling through Shepton Mallet when rain and hail began to beat against his car in such an angry way that he hurried into Cannard's Grave Inn and asked for a bed for the night. It must have been only a short time before closing when he arrived at the inn for it was, he said, emptying of customers. The inn, he maintained, had always held a fascination for him. He had passed it on several occasions but he had never been in it before. Being on his own he began to read a little of its history as he sat down beside the fire, warming himself with a good stiff brandy. He must have gone off to sleep very quickly and then only for a moment or so, and as he awoke with a start he found his brandy glass was just beginning to slip from his grasp. On opening his eyes fully and looking round him he saw a lady sitting on the other side of the fireplace, who had not been there when he first sat down. As she looked so strange and ethereal he could not, for what seemed a long time, say anything to her for he could not decide whether she was real or a ghost, so strange did she appear to him. Was she another wayside traveller come to rest awhile from the downpour outside, or had she come over to share his companionship . . . or indeed was he still dreaming?

'This is a lovely, warm and cosy inn,' he said to her eventually, just to break the stillness, and to see whether she was real.

'Oh, it is,' she replied. 'It is much better now than it was in MY day.'

He was startled by this disclosure, he said, for whatever could she mean by saying 'in my day', when she looked not a day older than himself?

'In MY day?' he asked incredulously . . . but she went on as though she had not heard him.

'You see,' she said, 'my husband Giles Cannard was the landlord of this inn. Every coachman in the country once knew of Giles Cannard as the most well-known and respected man from Weymouth to Bristol. As a husband also he was loving and loyal. One could never have envisaged that he could have changed in character so much over the years. Slowly and almost imperceptibly the man I first knew became an entirely different person, degraded, debased and disgraced.

'However, in due course, becoming aware that I had not many days to live, I called him to my side to ask him one last request before I died. I pleaded with him to reject the way of life to which he had subjected himself, and restore himself to his former years when we were both radiantly happy together. So touched was he by my request that, with tears running down his cheeks, he knelt beside my bed and, with his hand on his heart, vowed he would never again say or do anything he knew I disliked. Convinced that he was telling the truth, I calmly kissed him on both cheeks, and then, at peace with the world, I was borne upwards and passed into eternity. But he did not keep his promise.

And soon a shady deal made me aware
He needed help, which made me then decide
To come back from the dead, to make him see
The promise he had made before I died.

But then through shame or fright or misery
Or infamy he could no longer hide,
In uncontrollable fright he ran from me
And without thought commited suicide.

His body was interred without delay
Outside the corner window, on the green;
And ever since that most dramatic day
A macabre apparition's to be seen.'

My friend said he was so startled by this uncalled-for disclosure that, for a time, he did not know what to do. Continuing his story he went on to say, 'After Kate had finished talking, she disappeared before my very eyes, and I found myself all alone in the inn. I shuddered.

> I drank my brandy, then went out to see
> The very clouds above, the lonely lane:
> All she had said was true, as true could be,
> And loneliness o'erwhelmed me in its train.
>
> I am not usually scared, yet to my shame
> I had begun to turn as cold as ice;
> An eeriness enveloped my whole frame
> And held me in its stony, clammy vice.
>
> I tore myself away and ran inside.
> And took myself to bed and turned the key;
> For hours and hours to go to sleep I tried
> But ghosts of Kate and Giles prevented me.'

There have been many theories advanced to deny all that I have told you concerning Giles Cannard and Cannard's Grave Inn and as Giles lived such a long time ago one can understand why doubts should arise. However, I think another report of occurrences that took place at Cannard's Grave Inn, originally published by Aris's *Birmingham Gazette* on 12 May 1794, will confirm the truth of the story I have told you and will also give credence to the story of my friend's meeting with Kate Cannard a few years ago.

> The other Friday three gentlemen called at Cannard's Grave Inn and ordered a bottle of sherry wine; they drank considerably more than half but, disliking the taste, left the remainder and went away. Shortly after Miss B. (the daughter

> of the landlord) and the cook, being much fatigued with the labours of the day, indulged themselves with a glass each of the remaining wine. In less than ten minutes Miss B. was taken ill but recovered. The poor cook was not so fortunate. She found herself indisposed at the same time and on the Sunday morning expired in the greatest agonies. An inquest was taken at which three surgeons attended, and the jury returned a verdict that the deceased died through the effects of the wine.
>
> I believe the landlord of the inn in 1794 was William Beale, and I presume that Miss B. of this report was Miss Beale, but what is the explanation of the poisoned wine? Was it an accidental occurrence? Or was the landlord of 1794 falling into the evil ways of his predecessor of 150 or more years before? Who can say?

So ends the comment from the *Birmingham Gazette* and I now leave you to believe what you will. I must say in conclusion that Cannard's Grave Inn caught fire in 1980 and for many months remained a mere shell. It has now been restored into a three-storeyed building, retaining something of its original shape. The seventeenth-century original doorway, which has now a preservation order on it, has been re-erected on the west side of the new building. The greensward in front of the building under which Giles Cannard was interred has now been cleared in order to widen the road at the corner.

MARY'S GRAVE

Chantry is a scattered parish just off the A361 road from Shepton Mallet to Frome, consisting of four groups of houses: Chantry, Little Elm, Bull's Green and Dead Woman's Bottom. There is also a sinister Murder Combe and a Mary's Grave in the vicinity. Like most of these graves at the crossroads, where something sinister if not evil is said to lurk, Dead Woman's Bottom and Mary's grave are no exception. Of course, there have been exaggerations and additions to the actual event of that never forgotten night about which I am to tell you, but that is inevitable. Howbeit, it is not in me to give other than the unvarnished truth but, even so, it does not in any way make the events less sinister and, certainly, does not diminish the idea of the supernatural or paranormal activity. Facts are sometimes stranger than fiction.

When a young lady came to live at Bull's Green in about 1850, she appeared, to young and old alike, as something out this world. She had a wonderful and powerful presence, she walked with a certain air of sophistication and was always delicately dressed. She had lovely big eyes, which not only took in all about her, but also captivated all those who looked into them. Her golden hair was thick and alive and fell in billowy folds over her shoulders, and her skin was as soft as velvet. Where she came from no one seemed to know, and not one person appeared to take the trouble to ask. But very soon she was universally spoken of, and was the centre of conversation wherever two or three were gathered together.

It is said that when she went to a fair at Whatley on her first visit, interest in all other things melted into nothingness compared with catching a glimpse of her. And yet, it must be said, she never flaunted herself or went out of her way to attract others. She simply possessed a natural charm which, if I may use the term, bewitched people. Just to hear her say 'Good Morning' or 'Good Afternoon', accompanied by an unrestricted smile, was to see and hear the exceptional.

Obviously people, and especially men, were soon finding excuses to go to her door. All of them were entertained in a perfectly refined manner. Never was there anything unbecoming in her conduct to give the least impression she was less than ladylike. In fact, she behaved so perfectly that every gentleman who went to her door, on whatever pretext, was soon made

The church at Whatley in the parish of Chantry. Mary's ghost was said to walk the lanes near here looking for a place to lie in sacred ground

aware of it. Mary, for that was her name, was the perfect lady, unadulterated in every way. But the ladies in the village would have none of it. They assumed, and wanted to assume, otherwise.

In due course one gentleman, by the name of Frank, from the Vallis region of Frome, began to take an especial interest in her, and, it must be said, she a more than common interest in him. But his visits were not veiled in secrecy, for neither of them had anything to hide. However, it did not take long for the local ladies to find out who he was. They soon learned whence he came, his local interests, his opulence, and that he was married. Moreover, they knew that his wife was stupid and incapable of doing things for herself – a quite unreliable and incompetent person. Since Mary was not wholly welcome in the village, and therefore had little conversation with other people, she had not accumulated these facts. She had never asked Frank whether he was married, and he had never thought it necessary to inform her.

Although the authorities had registered Frank's wife as stupid, she was neither sufficiently insane to be put away nor sufficiently deranged to fail to see a change in her husband's demeanour. She noticed that something had happened in his life that had changed him completely. He was kinder to her than usual and was more considerate than he had been for a long time, as though he were compensating for doing something he shouldn't . . . like going out more in the evenings than he had done for many years. He had changed; and she was going to find out the reason, and by question and answer she was soon able to put her pieces together.

One autumn night, if I remember rightly 20 October, when the rain was beating down and the wind very strong, Frank, against all reason, decided to go out. Soon after he had gone, his wife, disguising herself, went out into the stormy night also. She walked all the way from Frome to Bull's Green and waited outside Mary's house in the shelter of an old barn. After an hour or so the front door of Mary's cottage opened and the old lady saw her husband depart. This wily woman had gathered her facts correctly! As soon as the horse's footsteps had died away, she knocked gently on Mary's door and Mary, assuming for some reason that Frank had returned, opened it, only to be confronted with a vicious woman standing in the doorway.

Early in the morning of Thursday 21 October a farmer was riding in the valley between Murtry Hill, just north of Murder Combe, when he saw a lady huddled up near some rocks protruding from the hillside. Considering it none of his business, he approached her only tentatively until he noticed blood on the rock as well as on the woman's hair. Leaving caution aside, he dismounted to obtain a closer view and found, without doubt, that she had been dead for some time. Very soon a constable and a doctor were at the scene. It was also early on the same day that Frank, having noticed his wife was missing, reported the loss to the constable at Frome and very soon, much to Frank's amazement, he was being asked to certify the dead woman as his wife. But the constable and the doctor were surprised to see strands of golden hair in the dead woman's clenched fist and pieces of skin caught in her long finger-nails. When Frank had been given this information he informed the constable he had grave suspicions, and asked the constable to follow him. As fast as their horses would carry them they rode to Bull's Green, and entered the open door of Mary's cottage to see the prostrate lady lying in a pool of blood, surrounded by upturned chairs, broken china and smashed pictures. From the wanton destruction they saw in the room, it was obvious that either a madman or a ruthless criminal had been abroad, and when they turned over the body they saw something which proved their fears to be true. Mary's face had been scratched as though by rats, making the erstwhile charming face almost unrecognizable, and her right eye had been torn from its socket. It was a diabolical and heinous sight which could only have been committed by a vicious, deranged and jealous person.

Frank had nothing to confess, apart from the fact that he had been visiting Mary. But the facts he told the magistrates, coupled with the golden hair and skin found on his wife's body, were sufficient to bring in a verdict of murder. Mary had been murdered by Frank's wife while her mind was deranged. But so cruel was the criticism of Mary by the village folk that she, who had done nothing amiss and was as pure as the driven snow, was denied a burial in sacred ground, even against the rector's advice. Such was the bitterness of evil tongues. It took a very long time to forget all that had happened on the night of Wednesday 20 October. There were the newspaper reports, the post-mortems, the rumours and the bitterness, but gradually peace settled once more in the little hamlets around Whatley and Chantry.

Then, some twelve months afterwards, when a couple named Harry and Florence were walking home from a dance, Florence reported having seen a lady in white walking along Murtry Hill. As soon as this was made public, many other women came forward and announced that they too had seen a lady in white. One confessed that she had been so close to her, that the lady in white turned and looked at her, and smiled in such a charming way that she was convinced that it was none other than Mary who once lived in Bull's Green. Still another spoke of her as having golden hair and lovely eyes, for both shone up even in the dark, and although she did smile in a most charming way, there was a little sadness about the face.

I often wonder whether it was Mary . . . and I wonder whether the sadness was due to the fact that she was still looking for a place to lie in sacred ground. Her grave can still be seen at the crossroads just outside Chantry.

The coppice at the crossroads, where Mary's grave can still be seen

MOLLY HUNT

Were you to read an Ordnance Survey map, you would see that between Cricket Malherbie and Dowlish Wake, near where the unclassified road from Wadeford to Kingston crosses over, lies the body of a certain Molly Hunt. People seem unsure who she was, some believing her to be a witch, while others speak of her as a prostitute. She was neither of these things. It is a very sad story, but in no case unusual.

Molly was the only daughter of Mr and Mrs Hunt who lived in a little cottage at Cricket Malherbie in a bygone century. The parents doted on her. Molly was their life, their expression, their every ambition. They had never taken into consideration that one day she would grow up, and wish to do things on her own. But she did grow up, and furthermore, grew into one of the most attractive girls in the neighbourhood. Young men were attracted to her as a moth to a candle and came from far and wide to get a glimpse of her.

Very soon her parents became worried about all the adoration that was shown her; consequently they could hardly bear her out of their sight. Mother, however, became more understanding and sympathetic to her daughter's longings as father became more and more excessively possessive, which prompted him to follow her wherever she went. If she went to Crewkerne he would find excuse to go. If she were going to a dance he would be there to take her home. He even enquired of those with whom she worked; the people to whom she spoke; those with whom she had her midday meal. Poor Molly's life became unbearable, and under father's constant gaze, she became secretive and morose whenever she was in his presence. It was such a pity, for she loved him just as much as he loved her. Of course, the situation was intolerable, and it was not long before things came to a head.

Now Molly had always been very particular about her habits. She was sincere, conscientious, loving and disciplined, intending at all times to follow a strictly moral code as she knew it. If only she had been allowed to take Frederick home it would have made all the difference in the world, but she knew it would never be allowed. Her mother had known that she was much attracted to Frederick, and had been seeing him for many months, but she dared not tell her husband. 'Oh, do be careful, Molly', her mother was frequently telling her. But the worst eventually came to the worst – Molly realized she was to have a baby. There was no doubt at all. But she did have doubts as to how her parents, and especially her father, would receive the news. The poor girl hardly knew what to do, although she knew she would have to tell them some time. There was no alternative. Eventually it was decided that Frederick should accompany Molly to her home and explain the position to Molly's parents and declare his intention of marrying their daughter.

Never had there been such chaos in that house before. There is no other way to describe it. Mr Hunt went raving mad. Against the pleadings of his wife, he beat Molly unmercifully and then tried to do the same to his wife and Frederick as they did all they could to tear Molly from his seemingly murderous grip. It was a frightening and unforgettable scene. Mrs Hunt said subsequently that she would never have believed that Mr Hunt could have said what he said, or have done as he did that evening. She had never thought him to have a temper. On the whole, she said, he was a moderate and loving man, who had always been the perfect husband and blameless father. He had just been overwhelmed by his own possessiveness and his one abiding love for his daughter to the exclusion of everything else; even to her growing up.

Molly never saw Frederick again after that evening, nor did she see her parents. The next day, on the pretence she was going to see her aunt, she kissed her mother, went out, and was found the next day in the River Ile. From the moment Mr Hunt was told of the tragedy he did not speak another word to his dying day. Mrs Hunt said that just before he passed away he did utter the word 'Molly' or, at least, that is what she thought he said.

Although no one in the area ever believed that Molly, lovely girl that she was, actually committed suicide, she was not granted a churchyard burial. She was instead buried at the crossroads between Dowlish Wake and Cricket Malherbie. Until recently flowers were constantly placed on her grave, a practice only ceasing because new hedgerows have eroded the grave area. No one was ever seen putting the flowers there. Some believe it was Frederick; some believe Mrs Hunt did so; but no one really knows.

The last time flowers were put on that spot, they were red carnations.

8: *Family Problems*

The Love Life of Sir Francis Drake. The Perfect Daughter. Clever's Daughter.

The Love Life of Sir Francis Drake

The first turning on the left after passing through Williton, on the way to Minehead, leads to Monksilver where the murdered Conibeer family, mentioned in the first chapter of this book, lie buried. Lying close to Monksilver is a sleepy little hamlet, containing four or five houses, including the grand old manor by the name of Combe Sydenham. The manor was built in the reign of Queen Elizabeth I by Sir George Sydenham, a high sheriff in the county of Somerset.

Now, born within these walls was a young girl, who was to become one of the most attractive and beautiful young ladies in the county. Being a maid of honour at Court, and the Sydenhams being one of the most influential families in the county, Elizabeth was soon brought into the presence of some of the most affluent families in the land. And it was not long before many promising young men came to seek her hand. One of those admirers was Sir Francis Drake, of Armada fame and Admiral of the British Navy.

Elizabeth fell deeply in love with him, but the course of true love was not as smooth as she may have wished. She, I am

Elizabeth Sydenham, whose love for Sir Francis never weakened

afraid, was not the only young lady in history whose parents would have preferred her to have married another. Their all pervading wish was that she should have fallen in love with a great friend of the family: the very rich and handsome Earl of Devon, Sir William Courtenay of Powderham. Elizabeth, however, was adamant, and would hear of no such thing. Her real love, her first love, her only love, was Drake. Whenever she was free from Court duty, and he was not sailing the seas in the *Golden Hind*, she spent all her time with Drake in London. Alternatively, he was in Combe Sydenham, probably playing bowls in the magnificent gardens surrounding her home.

Francis Drake, a man of undoubted knowledge, especially of his fellow men, must have been well aware that there were many other young men who had designs on Elizabeth. On one occasion, his anxieties being aroused when he knew he may have to be away longer than usual, he told Elizabeth that, if

Sir Francis Drake

during his absence, she should ever consider going to the altar with another, he, by God, would come between them by all the means in his power.

Week after week, month after month went by, the months eventually growing into years, without Elizabeth receiving any news from Drake at all. Feeling distraught by thoughts that she might never see him again, and being constantly reminded by her parents that that event was more than likely, her resolve if not her love, began to weaken, and she eventually gave way under the strain. She finally decided, much to the joy of her parents, to make preparations to marry Sir William Courtenay. Although she had changed her mind, it was obvious to her, and to many observers, that her heart was not wholly with Sir William.

As the horses passed through the village of Monksilver, along the winding lanes that led to the church of Stogumber where the wedding was to take place, her heart was still beating in tune with Drake. But the great procession of grey and white horses, knowing nothing of Elizabeth's thoughts, wended their way through the lanes, taking the groom and bride to their wedding.

In that fascinating, narrow street, in which stands the magnificent church, the first carriages drew to the side of the road, to allow the two chief carriages to go forward and pull up alongside the church. The groom with his best man alighted from his carriage; the attractive bride, holding on to her father's arm alighted from hers. Then everyone, guests, villagers, and those who had come from far, rushed forward to see Elizabeth resplendent in her bridal gown. Never before had Stogumber witnessed such an array of dukes and princes, earls and princesses. London itself had come to the small village of Stogumber.

But at that thrilling moment, over the hustle and bustle and movement of horses and men, a whirring sound was heard above their heads. The noise grew louder and louder, sounding like the long menacing blast of a typhonic wind. Frightened and alarmed, as many as possible ran for cover, while others instinctively ducked their heads. Suddenly, to the bride's consternation, and everyone's amazement, a meteorite fell with a crash at Elizabeth's feet.

All were speechless. Everyone held their breath. No one knew what to say or do. But in Elizabeth's mind, so full of uncertainty, this meteorite was nothing less than a cannon ball from Drake's ship, the *Golden Hind*. Drake had come between them as he threatened he would.

Elizabeth did not go through with the marriage. She returned to Combe Sydenham and, on Drake's eventual return, married him in Stogumber church on 8 February 1585. For ten years Francis Drake and Elizabeth lived happily together despite his voyages and his long absences from these shores. However, in August, 1595, on board the *Golden Hind*, off the coast of South America, Francis Drake made his will, a passage from which reads:

> I bequeath to Dame Elizabeth, my wife, all my furniture, goods, implements and household stuff whatsoever standing and being within the doors of my mansion and the land and house of Buckland Abbey.

The cannon ball, which had proved such a happy omen for Elizabeth, was placed in a position of honour in the hall of Combe Sydenham where it was to remain forever. A legend surrounds it that, should it be removed, it would, of its own volition, roll back to the porch of the house. It is fair to mention that it was once an exhibit in Taunton Museum, but it has now returned to its former resting place. This meteorite, which experts claim it to be, weighs over 100 lbs and is the size of a football.

But there is another incident in this story of deep and affectionate love, which shows to what length the path of true love will run.

In the church of Stogumber, lies the tomb of Sir George Sydenham who died in 1598. He lies between two ladies, one of whom may have been his wife, while the other is his daughter Elizabeth, Lady Drake. Lady Drake was the only child to survive, and she outlived her father by only one year, dying in 1599. But at the time of her death, she was the wife of Sir William Courtenay, Earl of Devon, whom she had married after Drake's death in 1596.

Sir William, whose proposed marriage was brought to an abrupt end by the intervention of the meteorite (Drake's cannon ball), had waited through Drake's return; through the period of Elizabeth's marriage with Drake; for a convenient time after his death, and had then gone to Elizabeth, and declared once more his life-long love for her. Elizabeth consented to his request to marry him, and this time there was no intervention.

To those who are not yet convinced of the truth of this story the following may be of interest. In the *Sunday Observer* of 18 June 1927, a letter was written by a descendant of the Sydenhams as follows:

> In the Drake family and the Sydenhams it has always been held beyond controversy that Elizabeth Sydenham of Combe Sydenham in Somerset was very much in love with Drake but her father absolutely forbade the marriage. Drake swore in parting with her that she should marry no other, and if she stood at the Altar he would come between them. He

Stogumber church where a falling meteorite stopped the wedding of Elizabeth Sydenham and Sir William Courtenay. Elizabeth took the meteorite to be a sign that her real love, Sir Francis Drake, did not want the wedding to go ahead

went off on one of his buccaneering trips and was not heard of for six years, and her parents persuaded Elizabeth to marry William Courtenay of Powderham (who became her second husband). As she went up to the Altar, a fire ball came down from heaven and rolled between them, and she again refused to marry anybody but Drake, who, after a time re-appeared and whom she married. The stone ball was still at Combe Sydenham a few years ago, and I have not heard of its removal to Buckland, where Drake's Drum is still in existence.

The Perfect Daughter

The A368 Churchill to Bath road passes through West Harptree, a place of immense interest. Apart from the Norman church, rebuilt in 1865, there are other buildings of equal, if not more, appeal. The Tilley manor-house, although altered in 1659, has stood on the same site, beside the church, from the time of King Richard II (1377–99). Gourney Court, immediately opposite, is named after the Gourney family who held the manor from shortly after the Norman Conquest, until 1506. But there are things in West Harptree that capture the attention and imagination perhaps even more than these.

Living in the village many years ago were Robin and Elizabeth Brown. Although they were a delightful family, they had a tendency to keep themselves to themselves, probably due to the fact that Elizabeth was considered by some of the villagers to be psychic. They lived just off the present A368 road, near the Blue Bowl Inn and an old corn mill known as the Stratford Mill. The latter has been moved to make way for the Chew Valley Lake and I am told it now stands in the Blaise Castle grounds in Bristol.

Now Robin and Elizabeth had one child, a daughter by the name of Catherine, who was to them an almost perfect daughter, and upon whom they lavished all their love. Consequently they could hardly bear her out of their sight, which did not worry Catherine in the slightest when she was a young child. As she grew in years, however, she naturally began to resent this parental possessiveness, and started rebelling very gradually in many little ways. Not least of these concerned the hour at which she arrived home, which grew later and later each evening and annoyed her parents greatly. The crisis came one night when Catherine did not return at all.

This was the first time in their married life that Robin and Elizabeth had cause to worry, for theirs had been a happy marriage which had, until now, been wholly reflected by their daughter. Very soon neighbours were being phoned by the anxious parents; the police were informed; and relatives questioned. For hours Robin and Elizabeth searched every nook and cranny; every conceivable hiding place; every house where a friend of Catharine lived – all without success. By this time other people had joined in the search. And then, quite suddenly and mysteriously, Elizabeth, who had joined in the search as eagerly as anyone, said that she must go home to welcome Catherine on her return. Such a quick change of plan and the peculiar remark 'on her return', seemed very strange to Robin but, knowing Elizabeth as he did, he said nothing and consented to her going. What followed was remarkable.

Elizabeth, who had only been home some ten minutes and had just sat down for a cup of tea, saw, to her great relief and exaltation, Catherine slowly walking up the garden path. At first sight she was so excited she could hardly restrain herself, but when she saw that Catherine was drenched to the skin and could hardly walk, she rushed up to her as soon as she came through the front door. 'Where have you been?' she began asking, almost incoherently in her excited state of mind. 'Where have you been? You're very late; your father is out searching for you; we've been everywhere; why are you so wet?' Such was Elizabeth's outpouring of love and concern that she hardly realized what she was asking or saying or doing.

However, she stood aghast when Catherine said nothing in response. She just looked her mother in the face, brushed her aside and went upstairs to the bathroom.

For a long time Elizabeth could hear her daughter moving about, but thought it best not to interfere or ask any more questions. She had perhaps asked too many already. She was only too pleased her daughter was safe and was once more back with the family. When Robin came home later, borne down with the sad news that they had not only failed to find Catherine, but not a single trace of her whereabouts could be seen anywhere, his face lit up immediately when Elizabeth told him Catherine had come home and all was well.

'Well, where is she?' asked Robin excitedly, finding it almost impossible to contain himself.

'In the bathroom,' said Elizabeth smiling.

'Well, let us go up and see her,' said Robin'

'All right, but whatever you do,' commanded Elizabeth, 'do not scold her.'

But Catherine was not in the bathroom . . . and the next day she was found drowned just near the Stratford Mill. She had been dead some twenty-four hours.

Clever's Daughter

Even if one took a whole day taking in all the wonders that Wells Cathedral has to offer, I still think many exciting things would be missed. One day is surely insufficient. Would the visitor, for instance, see Bishop Bytton's tomb, a touch of which is the simplest and cheapest cure for toothache that I know? Would he also see, behind the high altar, a stone in memory of Clever Morris, AD 1726? This stone marks the resting place of a doctor who, like so many people, had domestic problems at a certain time of his life. It concerned his daughter, who was certainly not the only daughter to cause problems for her parents.

We know about Morris' worries firsthand, because he was one of those people who kept a diary. However, Clever Morris was buried inside the cathedral not because he was the budding author of a diary, but because he had a passion for music. He founded the Wells Music Club which met regularly in the Vicar's Hall. He was also a singer of some repute and played several musical instruments, including the organ upon which he was something of an authority.

The thing that was most likely to destroy Clever's peace of mind was not, however, any member of his orchestra, but the courtship of his daughter with a person whom he considered

The south aisle of Wells Cathedral. It was here that the Revd Samuel Hill conducted the secret marriage ceremony of Clever Morris' daughter

beneath their standards. Many parents have had to meet this problem, each, I suppose, taking a different point of view on how the subject should be tackled. At the beginning of the eighteenth century people did not study books on psychology, and when they were confronted with such a case to answer, it brought forth a categorical 'Yes' or 'No'. So far as Clever was concerned, the answer was a blunt 'No'.

There is a solution, however, that couples who do find themselves in such unhappy circumstances can turn to today, and indeed could turn to at the beginning of the eighteenth century. That solution was to find a parson who would marry them, whether father agreed or not, and in this case it was the Revd Samuel Hill who did just that. He performed the ceremony secretly in the cathedral, and furthermore, the cathedral sacrist gave the bride away.

Now Clever Morris, as we have already indicated, loved music, and there was nothing that he would have liked better than to have played the bridal march at his daughter's wedding – so long as she married the man of his choice. What he didn't like were poeple who did things behind his back, be they parsons, sacrists or anyone else. He therefore summoned the Dean and informed him what his underlings had been doing in his cathedral. The result was that the Revd Samuel Hill was 'prohibited from serving in the cathedral again on any pretext', and the sacrist was suspended for one year. Well, that is what happened to the cathedral staff, but what happened in the house of the Morris family? There were tears, and pleadings, and bewailings, but all to no avail. Morris turned his daughter out of the house and refused to see her again.

Obviously the womenfolk endeavoured, not weekly but daily, to make the man of the household change his mind, but for many months he was adamant. However, he records in his diary an event on 23 October 1719, which seemed to bring about a reconciliation:

My daughter Betty, with my wife, and Mrs Evans and all the maidservants, came into my chamber while I was putting on my clothes. I refused to see her and ordered her to be down, and going into my closet I shut the door. But she opened it and with abundance of begging and crying she forced me to beg God Almighty to bless her. And so my wife kept my daughter to dinner.

Reconciliation? I do not know.

9: *Phantoms*

The Phantom Stage-coach. The Phantom Hearse. The Charger at Nunney. The Ghost at the Window.

THE PHANTOM STAGE-COACH

I suppose during our lifetime most of us have read some Shakespeare. Even if we have not, I am certain we have read this passage from *King Richard II*, or at least have heard the words:

> This royal throne of kings, this sceptred isle,
> This earth of majesty, this seat of Mars,
> This other Eden, demi-paradise . . .
> This happy breed of men, this little world;
> This precious stone set in a silver sea.

Now, according to Shakespeare these words were spoken by John o'Gaunt, and it is said that John o'Gaunt, for a time, lived and owned land in Pawlett.

If we turn left off the A38 Bridgwater–Weston-super-Mare road, and then turn left at the post office in Pawlett, we will come into a road known as Gaunt Road, and it was from the family at the end of the road that it derived its name. It was Robert Gaunt, who in about the twelfth century, 'embanked from the sea a thousand acres', which have since been called 'Gaunt's Ham' or 'Pawlett's Ham'. In the fourteenth century these lands descended to John o'Gaunt, and the following is an extract of his will, 'I, John o'Gaunt, do give and bequeath from me and mine to thee and thine, all that portion of land known as Pawlett's Ham'.

And so Pawlett, a practically unknown place in Somerset, is joined hand in hand with both the twelfth and the fourteenth centuries. In fact, in that little hamlet, at the end of Gaunt Road, numbering only about four houses today, and where Gaunt Farm still stands, an old tombstone was recently unearthed, and it is quite probable a small Saxon church once stood on that spot.

At the end of Gaunt Road there is an extension, a continuation, which will take you down to the River Parrett. Near the bank of the river, beyond which you can see Combwich, there is a ruined building on the right hand side of the road. This was once a stage-coach inn, known as the White House. Before the days of the A38 turnpike road, in the days of the stage-coach, this was a very important junction for the West Country. For from here travellers would be taken by coach and horses to the White House inn. They would then be ferried across the River Parrett, and then take coach and horses from the Anchor inn at Combwich on the other side of the river, to travel to Devon and Cornwall. In fact, in those days, it was the only way to get to Devon and Cornwall from Weston-super-Mare. Obversely, were travellers coming from those two counties they would take coach and horses to the Anchor inn at Combwich, be ferried across the River Parrett, take coach and horses from the White House inn, and then travel on to Bristol, Glastonbury, or wherever they wished to go.

Now, it is said that on one dark and stormy night, when the rain was teeming down and slashing the horses' sides, and the wind was blowing a gale, a coach and horses was making its way down the Pawlett's Ham to the White House inn.

Suddenly a clap of thunder set the horses stampeding, and so dark was the night that no one, neither the driver nor passengers, noticed the inn. All crashed headlong into the river, when the waters closed in upon them, and neither the horses, coach nor passengers were ever seen again.

I cannot vouch for the truth of this, although I have been down that road at midnight just to soak in the atmosphere, but it is rumoured that every now and again a phantom stage-coach and horses drives headlong down that road. Of course there are some who consider it all a mere fabrication, an hallucination of the mind, but I have spoken with people who claim to have seen it. One of these, a farmer, told me he was down Pawlett's Ham at midnight with a friend, helping a cow that had been in labour when, to his bewilderment and consternation, he saw the phantom stage-coach, and this is how he put it to me:

We saw the coach approaching Gaunt's Farm, on the hill
  And its lights seemed to dance in the trees;
We could even hear screams from people inside
  Above the hooves and the wheels and the breeze;
While the coach bounded on ahead of the wind,
  Which the driver did naught to repel,
As he blew on his horn loud, cacophonous sounds
  As though blown by an inmate of hell.

The horses still galloped as though borne on by wings,
  Through their nostrils belched forth clouds of steam,
While the lights faded out inside of the coach
  Each time we heard passengers scream;
But what could we do? For our blood froze like ice,
  We were powerless before the onslaught;
Not a soul was about, no gates could we close,
  We lacked power to do what we ought.

We could now do no more than try save ourselves,
 So we threw ourselves down by a tree;
The eyes of the steeds seemed to stare far ahead
 Yet were making a bee-line for me;
The wheels spun around, but no brakes were applied,
 I saw driver and mate sitting there:
E'en now they both lashed at the horses' raw sides . . .
 And then all seemed to vanish in air.

The Phantom Hearse

I have spoken of Cutcombe in some other part of this book, and I am only mentioning it again because in some measure the story it has to tell is similar to that of 'The Phantom Stage-coach'. At Cutcombe there was no phantom stage-coach, but there was a phantom hearse.

To have encountered this phantom hearse of Cutcombe Hill was an experience to be reckoned with. Many, many people were frightened, nay alarmed, when they saw it sometimes as far as half a mile away, although they were never able to explain why it created such panic and fear. They could only repeat that so ghastly was the sight, that they never wished to go out unaccompanied at night-time again.

To encounter the hearse at close quarters was to experience the unexpected because it came upon one without any warning whatever. For you see, the wheels made no noise; the hooves were as though made of rubber; and the nodding plumes did not stir in the wind. It was always accompanied by a black hound, with eyes seemingly as big as saucers, its movement graceful and quiet, and its head never moving from one side to the other. In Somerset these hounds are known as Yeff hounds.

But awful as the hearse and cortège were, they never appeared to do any harm; it was merely a frightful experience, sufficient to make the whole body tremble with fright or freeze into immobility. In fact it has been said it was quite impossible to witness any other sight with such dread.

One night a farmer from Winsford, who had wined and dined freely at the local inn, said, during a heated conversation concerning the phantom hearse, that he considered the whole story was nothing more than rubbish. He stated that 'he had never seen anything worse than himself!' But just to prove that there was no such thing as a phantom hearse, he would drive his horse and gig, he said, down Cutcombe Hill, through the village itself, and travel all the way to Minehead.

The night was beastly. The farmer had not taken that into consideration when he made his challenge. Over the hot fire inside the inn, stimulated by a hearty good meal, and potent drinks, he had not realized the temperature of the world outside; how dark it was; how wild the wind; how wet the night. In fact, he had not thought at any depth about his challenge at all. It was probably the wine that had prompted the discussion. Nevertheless, he was a man of his word.

Very late that evening, the footman of the Luttrell Arms in Dunster went out to close the shutters against the prevailing wind, which had risen to gale force. As he surveyed the precincts of the hotel, he was astonished to see what appeared to be a wild horse, pulling a gig, galloping towards him up the main street. To avoid being crushed to death he dashed into the porch at the very moment the wild horse missed the Yarn Market just opposite the Luttrell Arms by no more than an inch. The horse was breathing hard; it seemed its eyes were protruding out of its head; and it was staring straight ahead impervious to anything that may have been in the way. But there was no driver. This was no phantom horse and gig, however. Both were tangible as one could see as they crashed headlong into a wall just beyond the Luttrell Arms.

It was not hard to unravel to whom the horse belonged. The footman had seen that horse over and over again on market days in Dunster . . . but where was the owner? That was the crucial question that had to be answered. He was eventually found flat on his face on the slopes of Cutcombe Hill. Although he lay unconscious for weeks, and people began to wonder whether he would ever recover, he did eventually get out of bed, but he was never the same person again. No one dared ask him what happened on that eventful night, and neither did he mention the incident himself. All I can say is that he never went out again unaccompanied at night-time. Never again after that night did he drink, nor argue about paranormal activities, and neither was the phantom hearse ever mentioned in his presence.

Well, what did happen to the driver that night? Some may say he fell out of his gig in a drunken stupor. Many may say he fell out of his gig when it hit an immovable object, and he was thrown flat on his face.

But the local people will tell you that it was the phantom hearse of Cutcombe Hill that had crossed his path on his ride that night. Well, who can tell? And who dare deny it?

The Charger at Nunney

No one can miss the fine old inn The George at Nunney, which lies just off the A361 Shepton Mallet–Frome road, for its splendid sign swings right across the road. Although this is not unique, it is very rare. Nunney is well worth a visit to see its church and its castle immediately opposite the church; a picture, indeed, of medieval England. As it was beginning to get dark when I was there on one occasion, I decided to find a bed for the night at the inn.

I don't know whether you have ever noticed it, but there is nearly always someone inside an inn who is very anxious to tell their story, and to whom better than a stranger. It is quite probable the local people had heard the story-teller's tales over

The church and castle at Nunney where the ghost of the troubled Colonel Prater is said to ride in full armour on his phantom black stallion

and over again, and were tired of him. Before I had taken a sip of my whisky Tom was beside me.

'You're a stranger here,' he said. He didn't ask whether I was, he knew. When I told him I was a stranger and had been to see the castle and the church, he said, 'Ah, the castle! The castle! It's a remarkable building, very old, the beginning of the fourteenth century, I believe. The Delameres rebuilt it, and one always thinks of the Delameres in connection with the castle, although the Pauletts owned it in the fifteenth century, and the Praters also lived there. But the Delameres are not, and have never been, any trouble to us . . . but the Praters . . .'

Here he stopped and looked at me questioningly, wondering whether I was taking it all in.

'But how can the Praters trouble you?' I asked.

Tom took a long drink as though the answer demanded much thought and concentration. Then, putting down his glass on the table, he began to tell me his story.

'Every now and again,' he said, 'generally late in the evening, a big black stallion is heard trotting down the main street. On it sits a man in armour, upright and alert, and yet restless, looking from side to side as though expecting someone or something to overtake him. It is said he always goes into the entrance of the castle, but no one has ever seen him come out.

'It is also said that the horse can be heard at night by those standing silently by the road. The sound they hear is of a horse galloping towards them, getting louder and louder the nearer and nearer it gets. Yet it never arrives. Then there is a momentary pause and the steps can be heard getting softer and softer as they gradually fade away in the distance, and then all is gone. But the most frightening sensation one has to endure is on those occasions when the stallion comes up to one unawares, making no noise at all.

'On one occasion I was going home, after having spent an hour or two at this inn. I remember quite well I was talking to myself in a happy frame of mind, and yet in rather meditative vein, when, to my surprise I felt a presence beside me. Eventually I looked to my right, for I had remained motionless for some time, when I saw a big, black stallion beside me, and mounted on its back a man in full armour. Both were looking straight ahead, as though I was not even there. A big, black dog was by the stallion's side, with its mouth wide open and its tongue hanging out. It eyes were of tremendous size, as big as saucers, and white. I could feel its hot breath as it passed me by. It was a frightening experience which I cannot fully explain. It was horrible, eerie, unearthly. 'It would have been made easier had the rider said something for, on the particular night of which I speak, the horse appeared so big and powerful, while I felt so puny and small beside it. It would have eased the situation if the rider had spoken. As it was, nothing was said, and I was left trembling, yet rooted to the ground.

'Then all was quiet . . . deathly quiet . . . and a cold chill ran through my whole body, and, although no harm came to me, I was quite immobilized until rider, horse and dog had passed out of sight. I never want that experience repeated, I can assure you.

'I am not the only one who has experienced this phenomenon. There are many who have had the same experience and who will tell you the same story.'

He took another long drink and as I put another before him, I asked, 'But what is the explanation?'

'I can't say,' he replied. 'The majority view is that it is the ghost of Colonel Prater, who so heroically defended the castle on behalf of the king during the Civil War, but who subsequently went over to the other side. It is said it is his troubled conscience that stirs him in his grave, and he comes back to the old place to see whether he can make amends.'

I have been back to Nunney on more than one occasion in the evening, but I have never had the privilege of meeting Colonel Prater's ghost. But to Tom, there was no doubt at all that it existed.

Nunney Castle. Its moat may be the deepest in England

The Ghost at the Window

Some people have always believed that the manor of Puriton, lying to the left of the A39 Dunball–Glastonbury road, was haunted, but this belief is merely laughed at and scorned by the sceptics and those who can believe only those things they can see and touch. However, let us investigate more fully.

One very cold, dark and blustery night, a maid sat alone in Puriton Manor when she thought she heard someone knocking on the door. Afraid to go to the door herself, she refused to answer it for a time, but the knocking persisted. Thinking now that one of the family may have returned without a key, she went to the door and opened it, only to find there was no one there. Closing it, she returned to the room and pulled her chair closer to the fire. All was so peaceful inside that she felt rather pleased she was on her own, and did not have to go outside to brave the elements. She could hear the rain beating on the window panes and the wind howling in the trees and in the rafters above. She put two extra logs on the fire and began to settle down for the night. And as she looked into the flames that roared up that great chimney, she began to feel the warmth soothing her whole body, making it extremely hard for her to keep open her eyes.

Suddenly she was aroused from her reverie by a loud scream that seemed to come from the very bowels of the earth. 'Whatever was that?' she cried aloud, as her heart began to beat like a drum, harder and harder, faster and faster, making her erstwhile warm body tremble like a leaf. And then it came again . . . a screech . . . a howl . . . which built up to a crescendo and petered out as if someone were being strangled and fighting for breath. It was a howl that seemed to come from the very depth of hell, and which entered into the very centre of her being. It was awful, beastly, devilish, frightful – there were no other words to describe it.

No owl, or rook, or fox could make a noise like that, she murmured to herself. Then what could it have been? The poor distraught girl was almost beside herelf. She shot glances in all directions to see whether the windows had been shuttered, the curtains drawn and the doors locked. She was pleased to see that the shutters on the big window on her right had been closed, but what of the window behind her? Yes, it was gaping wide into the night. She could even see the rain outside pouring down the window-panes, and shadows caused by the wind blowing the trees in the distance. Why ever had those shutters not been closed and the curtains drawn?

Again and again, she looked to that window as though drawn by a magnet, and the more she did so the more she froze in her seat. Fear was stripping her of her usual calmness. She felt her throat tighten, denying her freedom to breathe, while her tongue could utter no sound.

She tried, poor girl, to persuade herself she was imagining things as she sat alone before the fire. The screaming had ceased, but suddenly it came to her that, with the shutters being open, she presented a perfect picture to anyone outside, silhouetted as she was before the glowing fire. Gradually feeling more calm within herself, she began to move slowly towards the window to close the offending shutters. Then she saw, to her overwhelming amazement, a hand move slowly across the opening, with the thumb pointing to the ground, leaving long streaks from the top to the bottom of the window-pane. Although terrified she involuntarily rushed to the window, to unlatch the offending shutters, for she could not rest until she had done so. Then, again, she saw the hand move upwards and downwards with the thumb pointing to the ground and, as she heard a plaintive cry seemingly petering away in the distance, she crashed the shutters together.

The sun was shining through her bedroom window when she awoke next morning, and beside her bed sat the housekeeper with a bowl of steaming soup. The family, the housekeeper and the other maid had all returned home about the same time the previous evening, and had seen the unconscious Stella stretched out on the floor, with blood streaming from her forehead, where she had hit herself on the corner of the window-sill. She had been taken to bed and given a warming pan and an extra couple of blankets. But what had happened on the previous evening was the question that was on everyone's lips in the manor-house.

When Stella had recounted all that had taken place the previous evening the housekeeper said sympathetically that she surely must have been mistaken. She argued that she could have been frightened, being all on her own in that big house. The screams she had heard had probably been owls or foxes close at hand, or it could have been anything on such a night as that. What she had considered was someone's hand may have been no more than the branch of a shrub blowing in the wind . . . 'for the wind was very strong last night, you know!'

But when Stella eventually returned to the kitchen and repeated the same story to the other maid, she felt that she was far more understanding than the housekeeper.

'Why, yes,' said the maid, who had been told by her mother that the manor was once a priory, and a missing heiress, who had been murdered, was walled up there by Glastonbury monks. She, herself, had never given the matter another thought when she came to work at the manor for, in any case, she had always considered that all her mother told her concerning the missing heiress, was nothing more than a fairy tale.

But Stella was of a more sensitive nature than her colleague. She had no doubt whatsoever, that the screams she had heard came from a human being. And the hand and the pointed thumb she had seen was the hand of a human being. There was no doubt about it. She had not been fooled. She knew what she had seen. Later that day, on the pretence that she was going to dust some furniture, she actually went to make a minute inspection of the area where she had collapsed. She gave a sudden start when she saw quite clearly finger-marks on the window-pane. Furthermore, on closer inspection, she saw the rain had not adhered to those finger-marks, as though the fingers may have been smeared with grease when they had scratched the window-panes. But looking closer still, she saw it was not grease – how could it have been? – it was blood.

Without another thought she went to the housekeeper and gave in her notice. She would not stay in the house a moment longer than was necessary. Although the housekeeper did all she could to make her change her mind, Stella was adamant. No, she would not remain in that house a day longer than was necessary. She did, however, have to remain in service another two weeks, and once more during that period she suffered another such night. It was all so very similar: the knocking; the screeching; and the hand stretched out with the thumb pointing. What did it mean? Stella was no longer frightened. She had only another two days to stay, but the sight of the blood-stained finger on the window-pane of the manor-house of Puriton she never forgot. She told her story to all and sundry.

There had always been rumours about the haunting of the manor, but people laughed about it as something imaginary. These things were always seen, they said, when others were not present to verify their claims or corroborate the evidence.

Stella lived to a ripe old age. She was told in her eightieth year that building work of one sort or the other had started at the manor-house. Later it came to her notice that the owner was going to install new drains, for the old ones were blocked, and the rain-water, which could not get away from the building, was destroying the foundations. When the workmen had dug down deep enough they found that the old ducts were made of wood. These were in the nature of hollowed out tree trunks, and in one of these hollowed out tree trunks, they found the skeleton of a young lady.

There was no getting away from this. Here was fact. Here was something tangible; something one could touch and see.

This was not the romantic story of a distraught young lady, but the actual find of a workman, who knew nothing whatever of Stella's experience. Did the blood-stained fingers which tore at the window when Stella was alone in the manor-house belong, then, to this young lady? Was she, I wonder, asking for help? Or was it the ghost of someone indicating where the murdered victim had been placed? I do not suppose we will ever know. However, I have been told that since the skeleton had been found and re-interred in sacred ground, there have been no more screechings in the night, and no more blood-stained windows.

And that is very significant, for surely it goes to prove that the noises that Stella heard were not caused by owls, for the beech trees are still there, and no screeches are heard today.

10: *The Missing Ones*

Owen Parfitt. Martha and Pru. The Missing Heir.

OWEN PARFITT

Shepton Mallet, the sheep town, where the Mallets, the lords of the manor, once came to live, is now an industrial centre. It is also the town where Babycham is produced. Just outside Shepton Mallet is a place called Board Cross, where once Owen Parfitt came to live with his sister, towards the end of the eighteenth century.

Owen Parfitt, was in many ways, a quite unimportant person, but yet he still manages to remain with us, while other really outstanding people of Shepton Mallet have been forgotten with the passage of time. So far as we can gather Owen Parfitt started his working life as a boy apprentice to a tailor, but this bored him so much, he went hither and thither in search of adventure and what he considered a worthwhile livelihood. It is said he eventually went to sea, some saying he even became a pirate. It could well be true, for it is also said that when he subsequently came back to settle in Shepton Mallet, he brought a great deal of money with him. However, although he clung to the money he is supposed to have possessed, it was not much good for him, for a stroke very soon rendered him paralysed.

Board Cross, the home of Owen Parfitt and his sister. Owen disappeared in the eighteenth century, never to be seen again

From that day he became dependent on his old sister, Susannah, and a younger woman, Susanna Snook, who lived just across the way. Obviously Owen spent most of his time in bed, but when the sun shone the two ladies helped him down to an invalid's chair which they placed in front of the house.

Now in the morning of 6 June 1768, or as Collinson, the renowned Somerset historian, says, 1763, Parfitt was taken downstairs and placed in his invalid's chair at the front door of their home at Board Cross, which adjoined farmer George's field, and a greatcoat and blanket were draped over his shoulders and knees.

One source informs us that when Parfitt was told by a neighbour that a strange seafaring man had been in the district asking for his whereabouts, Parfitt was supposed to have turned an ashen white, but said nothing in reply. But many such stories were rumoured about him at that time. Nevertheless it is very hard to explain what happened in the few minutes between Susanna Snook placing him at his front door and returning, after having gone across the road to her home. On her return, the helpless, paralysed, very old man, had completely vanished. Some say he was only in his slippers. Certainly he had left his greatcoat on the back of the chair – but he had gone. It has been suggested he took all his money with him, if he had any, that is. But Owen Parfitt had gone; he had vanished; vanished for ever.

The general opinion at the time was that he had been spirited away by a supernatural agency, and to add to this belief, it is said a terrible storm, with thunder and lightning, suddenly burst over Board Cross, but this again may be no more than hearsay. No one seems to know. But history does relate that a most exhaustive search was made for him. Every wood, cavern, ditch, barn and well for miles around were searched with diligence and thoroughness, but all in vain.

It was suggested that some Bristol acquaintances of Parfitt's had expressed a desire to get rid of him, and that he had been carried off and murdered. But where was the body? To dispose of the body has always been the hardest thing for a murderer to accomplish. Furthermore, Susanna Snook was away from him for only a few minutes, and there were no speedy cars to whisk people away in those days. A widow, named Lockyer, a distant relative and a somewhat doubtful character, was also mentioned as having had something to do with his disappearance, but there was no proof relating to any of these suggestions.

Poor Susannah did not sleep for nights hoping for her brother's return, but he never did during her lifetime. For months and years rumours, threats and prosecutions were spoken of until gradually the rumours, threats and shouting passed away, but the memory of Owen Parfitt's disappearance remained.

Now it so happened that in 1813 (some fifty years after Parfitt's disappearance) a Mr Strode, inheriting some property at Board Cross only a hundred yards or so from Susanah Parfitt's old house, decided to make a few alterations to his property before moving in. He began his excavations close to the perimeter wall of his garden, when, to his surprise, he struck what he believed to be a stone, but which turned out to be a human skull.

One can imagine the result of such a find! But Mr Strode was not a man to lose HIS head easily! He quite rightly saw to it that the authorities were informed immediately and eventually a complete skeleton was discovered. Here was a climax indeed! Everyone waited with bated breath for the result of this find. Surely this was Owen Parfitt! Here was the missing man!

The skeleton was examined by an eminent anatomist, but within a few days, back came the news; disappointing news for those who were hoping it may have been Owen. In actual fact, it was the skeleton of a young woman.

Who she was no one seemed to know, for nothing more, so far as I can gather, was done about her. They didn't seem to prize life too dearly in those days. Or was it that the authorities were disappointed? So the fate of Owen Parfitt, the cripple who could hardly walk and yet could disappear within a few moments, still remained a tantalizing mystery.

Years later, when demolition work was being carried out at the beginning of this century near Board Cross, very close to where Susannah Parfitt's house once stood, a slab covering a well was found, which again raised hopes that the mystery of Owen Parfitt would be solved. In due course, under close observation, the slab was removed, the well was drained and thoroughly searched. Owen Parfitt's body was not found in the well. He still remained the mystery of Shepton Mallet.

Shepton Mallet church

A peaceful man or a pirate? Crippled or crooked? Was he murdered or did he run away? And if so, how and why? These are questions that remain unanswered. The only questions we can answer truthfully are that Owen Parfitt was real; he lived in Shepton Mallet; he began life as an apprentice tailor; he once lived at Board Cross in the home of his sister, from where he was whisked away in a moment of time, never to be seen again, living or dead. The mystery remains.

MARTHA AND PRU

The Drum and Monkey is an inn in the centre of Kenn, a village within two to three miles of Clevedon on the Yatton road.

For many years the inn was kept by a landlady, a very artful individual some people considered her for, whenever a travelling customer ordered his drink and proffered his money, Nellie was in the habit of saying she had no change. Eventually she was given the name 'Nellie No-change'.

However, as she was considered rather cunning, a highly commendable side of her character went unnoticed. Namely, she was the one lady in the village who befriended Pru when she was in dire need of help. Let me explain.

There was a little cottage in Kenn Street (it has recently been pulled down) where two sisters, Pru (her real name was Isabella) and Martha lived. As far as one can remember they had been resident in the village for ages, for no contemporaries even remember them coming. It was obvious therefore, they were very well known, even though they kept themselves to themselves, probably due to the fact that Pru was a little simple.

It was generally Martha who called on the other folk in the village, or went to the farm for produce, and it was she who did the buying when the grocery or butcher's van called at their cottage. However, it was a very happy household; Pru and Martha getting on well with one another, with Pru always obedient to Martha's orders.

But one day the village awakened to find that Martha had disappeared. Pru had called early in the morning at the local farm, to tell the farmer she had lost her sister, who had not returned home from her shopping expedition in Clevedon the previous day. Knowing that Pru was a little simple the report was not taken very seriously, until the news began to spread as subsequent investigations were made. Everyone's first thoughts were of Pru, and that is where 'Nellie No-change' came to the fore. She may have played artful to visitors in her inn, but she had a warm heart for most of the people in Kenn, and could not bear to think of Pru living all by herself in her little cottage. Consequently she decided to allow Pru to live at the inn for a few weeks, a period which actually turned into years. But what of Martha?

There are only a few clues to this unsolved mystery – for it still remains a mystery. We do know that on the day in question, Martha had walked to Clevedon, only some two or three miles away, for something she desperately wanted for the home, leaving Pru alone in the cottage. It is also a well known fact that Martha had come back from Clevedon, for on cycling home from Clevedon where he worked as a gardener, Fred Avis, a local man living at 'Dewsbury' in Kenn, saw Martha sitting on Stone Bow, a bridge which spanned the river in Kenn. He said he believed she was in good spirits, for she was singing to herself as he passed her. So we know she was not kidnapped in Clevedon, or murdered on the way home, for Fred Avis was a reliable witness.

'But she was singing,' said Fred. So could it have been that Martha had been drinking? This is doubtful, for she bought no liquor from the grocer, and neither did she frequent the Drum and Monkey in the village. She was, it is safe to assume, a total abstainer. But for some inexplicable reason and in a loose moment, she may have drunk on the day she disappeared and being unsteady, as she sat on Stone Bow, could have fallen into the river and drowned.

But the river was dredged thoroughly. So were the ponds and rhines, though all to no avail. Barns, granaries, houses were searched – but Martha was not found. She had disappeared into oblivion. One can understand someone getting lost in a crowded town or city – but how can one get lost in a village the size of Kenn? But Martha was never seen again dead or alive, even though the most exhaustive searches were made near and far. The disappearance of Martha Coles is the unsolved mystery of the village.

However, we are pleased to learn that 'Nellie No-change' cared for Pru until she died in 1940. Nellie forsook the inn, and later, she passed on too. There are some people who believe she appears at the Drum and Monkey, dressed in a black skirt, wearing a white apron, but I feel this is mere hearsay, and without any basis of fact.

The Missing Heir

Beside the A370 Weston-super-Mare–Bristol road lies a hamlet to the left of the road, known as Brockley. This was the home of the Smyth-Pigott family, who purchased the Brockley Estate as far back as 1661, and furthermore held it until 1914 when much of the outlying land was sold.

I have it on the authority of a gentleman who lives within a stone's throw of Brockley Court, that it has never been without its ghost. And to confirm what my gentleman friend says, he showed me an autobiography of Sir Reginald Kennedy-Cox, wherein he records that he was an undergraduate at Oxford at the same time as one of the Smyth-Piggott family. On one occasion he recalls a lecturer coming to the university to speak on the supernatural. He began his lecture by saying that he had 'yet to meet the man who had seen a ghost', to which Smyth-Pigott exclaimed, 'Meet him now, sir'.

Yes, Brockley Court has had its ghost for many years and my friend was kind enough to tell me what he believes was the origin.

One of the heirs of the Brockley Estates, he told me, had been in the forces stationed abroad for such a long time that it became uncertain whether he would ever wish to return to this country, let alone Brockley Court. It was thought that as his younger brother had proved himself an able administrator, and that the estate was progressing well in his hands, there was no urgency about his returning. It was quite probable that he preferred living in foreign climes. Since his absence had grown from months into years, the younger brother was also beginning to feel that his elder brother had no intention of returning. Probably he had been killed, he thought, for he had received no letter in reply to his own; what else could be the reason for his long absence? Furthermore, money that had been sent to him had never been acknowledged or returned. Where did it go?

Although Brockley has been described as 'a small village', it is, in actual fact, no more than a hamlet, which made it extremely unlikely that there were many alive who ever knew, or could remember, the heir to the estate. And the few who had worked for the family all their lives, and were now deeply concerned with the present squire's serious illness, considered the heir had forfeited his claim to the estate altogether. They were of the opinion that the young brother should automatically come into the title, as indeed he did.

Now, many years afterwards, when alterations were taking place in the Court, some of the workmen had cause to go down into the cellar which had apparently been sealed for many years. The only light the workmen had as they found their way through the rubbish stored below was by means of a torch, which, although it helped them to find a path through the debris, also produced macabre shadows which the workmen said were too horrible to behold. In fact, there appeared to be nothing to allow in light or even fresh air and there was such an unsavoury atmosphere about the whole place that some of the men refused to remain.

Two workmen, however, did remain, much to their dismay, for when they moved an old sack with its accumulation of dust and dirt, they saw, to their horror, a bare skull looking up at them through the rays of the torch. Disturbing the sack still more by means of a pole – they dared not touch it with their hands – they discovered a skeleton lying near the perimeter wall. Obviously, it was eventually handed over for examination by experts, whose only conclusion was that the skeleton was male. Although some people declared it must have been the remains of the heir to the estate, this was by no means the unanimous opinion. And it must be said in passing that no conclusion was ever reached as to how the skeleton arrived in the cellar, for it was clear it could not have arrived there of its own volition. Some evidence was provided by a man who said he remembered an army unit from abroad coming to stay in the Court grounds for a few days some years previously, setting up camp in a field behind. However, where the unit came from or who gave it authority was never satisfactorily established, according to my friend.

But he insists that that was the origin of Brockley Court being haunted, although he maintains that no one talks easily of hauntings these days.

11. Big *Men and* Strong

The Man with no Arms. Norton Malreward's Strong Man. Wedmore's Giant.

THE MAN WITH NO ARMS

I would like to tell you of a redoubtable man who has gone down into history by the name of William Kingston. He lived at Ditcheat, a village within a few miles of Shepton Mallet, and caused quite a stir in his day, both by his remarkable feats of strength and his ability to overcome difficulties.

On 25 February 1764, according to a family tree in the possession of Mrs Cecil Kingston of Mill Farm near East Pennard, Ann, the wife of D. Samuel Kingston, was delivered of a stout boy without arms or shoulders. Yet, according to Collinson, the renowned Somerset historian:

> he was in later life able to dress and undress himself, comb his own hair, shave his beard, clean his shoes, light a fire, and write out bills and accounts, accomplishing all these tasks with his toes. Being a farmer, he foddered his cattle, made his ricks, cut his hay, caught, saddled and bridled his horse with his feet and toes. He can lift ten pecks of beans with his teeth, with his feet he can throw a sledge hammer further than any other man with his arms, and has fought a

> good battle and come off victorious. Add to this he married a young woman of a reputable family. The above facts are truly authentic and notorious to this place and neighbourhood.

The historian Phelps added to this extraordinary account that the above description of himself was read over to the man Kingston some time after it was written, and was attested and verified by him in the following words:

> The above account is strictly true, and much more might have been added. Written by me with a pen of my own making, without hands or arms, Ditcheat, Somersetshire, June 16th, 1817. Testified, Bill Dawe, J.S. Cook, G.S. Dawe.

Perhaps one of Kingston's earliest and most famous exploits was the great battle he fought in 1789. Here is a contemporary report of this amazing fight, as it appeared in the *Western Flying Post* for 21 September of that year.

> Thursday s'sennight a battle was fought at Ditcheat, near Castle Cary, between Kingston, a young man born without arms, and Champion a blacksmith. The contest lasted half an hour during which time Kingston so well played his part, both with his head and heels, that his antagonist was taken off the field of battle with two broken ribs and a dislocation of his hip bone.

Kingston was at this time twenty-four years old.

About a year later the Revd John Wesley visited Ditcheat on one of his preaching tours of Somerset, when he wrote the following in his journal:

> Tuesday, August 31st, 1790, William Kingston, the man born without arms, came to see me of his own accord. He is

> of middling height and size, has a pleasing look and voice, and an easy agreeable behaviour. At breakfast he took off his shoes, which was made on purpose, took the teacup between his toes and the toast with his other foot. He likewise writes a fair hand, and does most things with his feet which we do with our hands.

In June 1790 Kingston married Miss Elizabeth Elford of Chetnole, Dorset and by her, he had seven daughters and one son. A very remarkable story is told of the way in which Kingston became acquainted with this lady.

A lady then living in or near London, had a remarkable dream that made a great impression upon her. She had a vision of an armless man who would be her husband. Her mother, obviously, tried to knock the whole idea out of her head as a foolish and superstitious notion, but in vain. To understand the following we must remember there were no cattle trucks in those days, so that cattle from places in Somerset would be driven by road to their destination. The young lady who had had the vision was, one day, looking out of her window, when she saw a large herd of cattle passing the residence in which she was staying with her mother. To her astonishment she saw that the man who was driving them was without arms. She shouted to her mother that her husband was in the street, and rushed out and invited the man to come to her home, when his work had been completed. Eventually she became his wife.

In 1810 Kingston's wife died, but notwithstanding he had numerous daughters, he was not content to remain a widower. In the following year he married Elizabeth Ashman, by whom he had two sons and two daughters. It is recorded that the wedding was attended by an immense concourse of people who were delighted at the manner in which Kingston took the hand of his wife and placed the ring on her finger and signed the register with his feet.

Kingston's children are said to have all been normal and well-developed. Their descendants, some of whom I have had the privilege of meeting, namely Bernard and Christopher, both sons of Mrs Kingston (and Mr Cecil, now deceased), are still living in the district.

Norton Malreward's Strong Man

I think I have only ever seen one signpost pointing in the direction of Norton Malreward. I therefore feel you may not find it easy to get there. Probably the easiest way is to begin at Dundry, a village on the right of the A38 Churchill–Bristol road, immediately after passing the road that leads to Long Ashton beside the reservoirs on the left.

In Dundry itself, we must leave the magnificent towered church on our left, pass some new bungalows on the same side of the road, and continue until we come to crossroads. Here we should cross over, and drive slowly along a lonely, hilly road, which will take us to Bristol and Whitchurch if we are not careful. However, after passing Ivy Farm, we should take the first turning on our right. There is no signpost.

But however difficult to find, we must go there, because it is a place of giants, if we are to believe what we are told. Just before we approach Norton Malreward down in the valley, there is, over on our right, the Iron Age earthworks of Maes Knoll Fort, which is of great interest from many points of view, as we shall soon learn.

On reaching the village at the bottom of the hill, we should first go into the church, passing the very large ancient yew in the churchyard. From here we can see the Georgian manor-house, with its Ionic and Tuscan pilasters across the way. The church, largely rebuilt towards the end of the seventeenth century, contains a fine Norman arch and a thirteenth-century tower which are the oldest parts of the building.

Although it is said the name 'Malreward' is derived from a family of that name who lived in the vicinity, there are not many people who will accept this theory. The great majority of people seem to favour another interpretation. This concerns Sir John Hautville, a giant of a man, who lived in Norton Hautville (now Norman Hawkfield), where he performed amazing feats of strength.

King Edward I, having heard of his amazing physique when visiting the neighbourhood, supposedly asked Sir John to give a demonstration of his powers. Sir John thereupon took aside three of the king's heaviest soldiers and dexterously put one under each arm, taking the third between his teeth and then attempted to climb the steps of the church's tower. All went well until the soldiers became restless, when Sir John crushed them in his arms.

For this feat of strength the king gave Sir John the land of the parish. However, it is rumoured that he was a little displeased with the gift, which he thought was a 'bad' or 'mal'

The effigy of Sir John Hautville, in Chew Magna church. Sir John was described as 'a giant of a man' who performed amazing feats of strength

reward for his efforts – hence the name Norton Malreward. In fact, so disappointed was Sir John that he is reported to have climbed to the top of Maes Knoll and hurled a huge stone from the summit, which landed a mile away in a field beside Quoit Farm on the road to Stanton Drew. And to those who believe this story to be far-fetched, I can assure them that the stone is still there beneath the horse-chestnut trees. It is known as 'Hautville's Quoit'.

Sir John is said to have been buried in the church of Norton Malreward, but when a part of the church was demolished during the rebuilding process, his wooden effigy was transferred to the church of Chew Magna.

Wedmore's Giant

One night, many years ago, when Mr and Mrs Harry Green of Wisteria Lodge in Wedmore came out of their friend's house in Axbridge, just off the Weston-super-Mare–Wells road, to return home, they were confronted with an awful decision. One part of the better road, which would probably be our B3151 today, had been dug up owing to recent flooding, and was therefore impassable. This meant the road through the moors was the only alternative. The night was pitch black and a fog lay dense all over the moors. There was one saving grace, however, according to Harry Green, and that was that the very high wind occasionally cleared the fog sufficiently for one to be able to see the way ahead, at least for a few moments at a time. The only other thing that worried him at all was the fact that he had brought out that day his more sensitive horse called Floss, who was, at times, quite troublesome. But on the positive side, he had with him his faithful dog, Collie, who had the knack of negotiating the moor roads, even in the dark. Against all the advice of his friends, and the promptings of his wife, he decided to make the journey. It was not far, he said, even if he had to walk all the way, and both he and his wife were well prepared for a wet and tiresome journey.

With the frequent clearings in the fog they managed far better than they had expected, and Mr Green was very pleased he had made the decision to move. The journey up to the turn of the road had been without peril, and they had moved very quickly considering the numerous problems they had envisaged before setting out.

But within 2 or 3 miles of Wedmore, so Mr Green subsequently related, the dog became uneasy. First it would stretch itself, and then relax, almost as though it was throwing a fit. Moreover, this started just as the fog had begun to fall again making progress at this juncture very slow indeed.

'I got out of my cart at this point,' said Harry, 'because I could begin to sense something eerie myself, just at the very moment that Floss began to shy and quiver like a leaf. By the time I had managed to get hold of her bridle, she became almost impossible to handle, and I was dreadfully afraid she would bolt with my wife helpless in the cart. However, I managed to calm her down eventually.

'When all was quiet again, my wife whispered to me that there was someone in front, standing in the middle of the road, standing, so it seemed, as high as the willows. "Be reasonable, Kate," I said, "how can one stand as high as a tree, and in any case, what would he be doing here in the middle of the road at this time of night?" But before I could confirm her statement, the fog had thrown a thick pall over the area, and I could not see more than a yard before me.

'However, with the ground feeling hard beneath my feet, I was determined to move on, but the horse was not of the same mind. He would not budge. His eyes were bulging; hot breath was coming from his nostrils; he was stamping the ground in an uncontrollable manner. At the same time, the dog had begun once more to growl and whine even louder than ever, and my wife had begun to scream. It was all so very horrible. If

I had been drowning in a deep morass I could not have felt more helpless. There seemed to be nothing I could do. I threatened, I shouted, I soothed, but I seemed incapable of controlling the animals, and my wife. And then – it was hard to believe such things could happen – I saw, standing in front of me, beside the horse and cart, a grinning man, looking down upon me. I say, looking down, because he must have been some 7 to 9 ft tall. He appeared to me tremendous and horrendous. I can still see him to this day.

'He stood there with a hideous grin on his face, showing teeth resembling those of a gorilla. He also stood like one, his arms akimbo, as though he were about to lift the horse and cart (and it seemed quite possible for him to do this) and throw us into the swamp.

'All I had with which to defend myself and my wife was my whip, and accompanied with one piercing scream, and with the last ounce of strength I could muster, I slashed the whip across his body. But the whip didn't stop as it made contact. It went straight through him, and it was only then that I realized I was in the presence of something paranormal, a ghost, a phantom, or whatever you like to call it.

'Before I could get on to the cart to strike again, because even now, in my particular mental state, I was not certain what I had encountered, the phantom or ghost disappeared.'

After that sudden, inexplicable and awful occurrence, Mr Green was able to negotiate the rest of the journey, put the horse in the stable, revive his wife with brandy, and get to bed in the early hours of the morning.

Although it was late before he got to bed, he was up as soon as it was light, going to the place where he had encountered the ghost the night before. He knew he would be able to locate the spot because of the willow trees, and the great indentation in the verge, into which he had fallen when alighting from the cart. Mr Green had not been dreaming. There in the middle of the road were scratchings and deep marks, and loose stones on the surface of the road made by the frightened horse. And there was the great hole in the verge where he had fallen. There was no doubt about it at all – something of a peculiar nature had happened that night.

Now, when I first heard this story, I had grave doubts as to its credibility. I do in no way disagree with people who say they have seen ghosts or been in haunted houses. There are too many people, and intellectual people as well, who declare they have seen ghosts, for me to reject their stories out of hand. But giants standing 7 to 9 ft tall, this was surely too much of a story to believe.

Genesis, the first book in the Bible, says, 'There were giants on the earth in those days' (Genesis 6: 4), but surely not in Wedmore in the eighteenth century? Then one day I picked up a section of the enormous *History of Somerset* by Collinson, who is the great accepted authority on Somerset, and this is what I read:

> In sinking a well, in some part of the parish of Wedmore in the year 1670, there was found at the depth of 13 feet, the remains (as a certain antiquary will have it – probably Gibbons) of one of the Cangick giants, a people supposed to have formerly inhabited these parts. The top of his skull was said to be an inch thick, and one of this teeth 3 inches long above the roots; 3½ inches round, and after the root was broken off, it weighed 3½ ounces.

A mystery indeed!

12: Haunted Houses and Churches

Sidcot's Poltergeist. Christmas Carols. The Haunted Chapel. The Haunted Gateway.

SIDCOT'S POLTERGEIST

Just off the A38 Bridgwater–Bristol road, there once stood a small cottage beside the Quaker Meeting-house, which was founded in 1699. The small cottage was the home of George Beecham, a cattle doctor, and his wife. When George Beecham lay dying (we know little of what he did before this) he told his wife to bury him, not in consecrated ground, but in his own garden, so that as he lay in his grave he might have the amusement of watching people as they passed by. 'Now, if you don't,' concluded the old man, 'I'll come and trouble 'ee.'

His wife, although always anxious to please her husband, had to prevaricate on this occasion, for she believed it was wrong not be buried in consecrated ground. So on 27 July 1788, the parish register informs us that his remains were deposited in Winscombe churchyard.

A year passed by and on 22 July, twelve months to the day that George had departed this life, the Sidcot Quakers were sitting in their quaint little building over the way, when the solemn silence was broken by the voice of a terrified woman. 'Do please come,' she said, ' all my things are falling about the floor,' or, to translate it into Somerset dialect, 'Oh, neighbours, do 'ee come! Here be all widow Beecham's things a-valling about the vloor!'

Two of the Quakers, John Banwell the headmaster, and Charles Strode, immediately went to the widow's cottage where they saw chairs and tables, pots and pans dancing about the room and the kneading trough rocking to and fro as if moved by invisible hands. And when the onlookers saw the dead man's boots clattering slowly downstairs into the kitchen they stood aghast. The two men could find no solution to the mystery. As the disturbances were still continuing in the Beecham's cottage after the meeting was over, they brought other Quakers to see what was happening. Among these was Hannah, the headmaster's daughter. Subsequently, Mrs Hannah Frank used to describe how she had to move out of the way to avoid a large armchair that was slowly moving across the room.

Hannah More, the philanthropist, is said to have driven over from Cowslip Green at Wrington to enquire into the circumstances, and Mr Jones, the editor of *Mendip Annals*, then curate and afterwards rector of Shipham, and teacher of French in John Banwell's school, also visited widow Beecham's cottage to investigate. They were both at a loss to explain what they saw.

Here is a case of the paranormal being seen by many witnesses, among whom were men of no mean intelligence. However, I suppose that people who can only believe those things they can see and touch will not be persuaded even by the veracity of this incident.

Jone Beecham, as her name is spelt in the burial register, survived her husband by six years. But he did not trouble her again.

CHRISTMAS CAROLS

There is a fascinating village, known as Stanton Drew, lying to the left of the A37 Farrington Gurney–Bristol road. There is another story about Stanton Drew in this book, but, for the present, I would like you to come with me to see a group of private dwellings known as the Cottage, the Little Cottage and Fern Cottage adjoining one another. I am afraid, however, we cannot go into them, for they are all occupied. The Cottage is now the home of Dr J.P. and Mrs Telling.

Originally these buildings were part of a monastery, but whether this is the reason some people, even today, have experienced strange phenomena in their houses, we cannot say. Certainly many people have, at different times, had experiences in the Cottage and the Little Cottage which defy logical explanation.

Visitors to Stanton Drew, who are always welcomed by the local people, chiefly come in the summer months to see 'The Stones', but these visitors are few and far between in the winter, which allows the locals to carry on their normal pursuits unheeded. The few weeks before Christmas are always exceptionally busy, as they are in most places. Preparations are being made for home-comings, and arrangements are underway for social functions in individual homes and in the village itself. Extra choir practices are taking place at the church; nativity plays are being rehearsed in school, while the companologists begin practising their handbell ringing once again to enable them to be doubly proficient when they call on residents to play carols.

Mrs Lynton, who had lived at the Cottage for forty years before the Tellings came to live there, was not unlike the rest of the people in the village. On one particular Christmas she was looking forward to hearing carols being played once more on the handbells in her home. She had already prepared the glasses of sherry in her spacious drawing-room, and had placed fancy cakes and mince pies on the sideboard for the ringers, and she had stirred the fire so well that already flames were leaping up the chimney. Consequently, when the ringers came, the room was warm and inviting, and she was soon in her seventh heaven, sitting in her armchair listening to the music of the bells. It was just like the days when she was a child at home with her parents. It was so lovely to reminisce while listening to the old carols, 'See amid the winter snow' and 'O little town of Bethlehem'. What more could one ask? The fire crackled . . . the ringers played on . . . and on. . . .

Suddenly Mrs Lynton froze in her seat and everyone was rudely awakened as there came a thunderous banging on the front door. It was not the gentle knock of a neighbour calling for attention, or one wishing to gain admission – it was a crash as though a coach had driven through the front of the house. Mrs Lynton was not the only one to be alarmed and startled. The bell ringers, trembling as they replaced the bells, made for the front door in a frenzy. They were startled again when they found the door locked and that no damage had been done. But what astonished them more than anything else was that there was no one at the front door, and not a person in sight. There seemed to be no explanation. But the atmosphere was now so tense, and the interruption so mysterious, that the bell ringers, when they came back to gather their bells, were so stunned and frightened that they were almost incapable of controlling their movements. It was a sad end to what had promised to be a glorious evening.

When her guests had departed Mrs Lynton did not take long to recover her composure, for having reflected on the mysterious poltergeist (if that was what it was) she remembered she had had experiences before of what may be termed the paranormal. Many times, when living in her upstairs room, she had felt the presence of someone near her which she could never explain. So real was this presence that, when it moved, she could follow the direction of the ghost or apparition as it made its way across the room. She affirmed she saw nothing herself, apart from what appeared to be an invisible wind blowing from the wall to the door, and to prove her sanity, her two dogs, hackles raised, followed the line along which the apparition moved. But Mrs Lynton had never come to any harm, and so, with a shudder, a smile, a sherry in her hand and her dogs on her knees, she tried to forget the whole sequence of events, however disturbing they may have been.

Martin Telling, the son of Dr Telling, the present owner of the Cottage, told me he had had a similar experience to that of Mrs Lynton as late as 1985, when being alone in the house, he heard the crashing of the front door, to which he rushed with all haste, only to find the door locked and not a soul in sight.

He also affirms that before the Cottage was completely redecorated, after his parents had purchased the house, he, for a time, slept at the Little Cottage which stands in between the Cottage and Fern Cottage. On four occasions, he maintains, on waking in the middle of the night, he could hear children talking, and he confirms this story by saying that on one occasion a friend of his slept there and had a similar experience. But there were no children living or even staying at the Little Cottage, or in the cottages on either side.

THE HAUNTED CHAPEL

One of the oldest places in Keynsham is the church of St John which was begun in 1292. A hideous storm in 1632 caused the tower to collapse when the nave and the aisles were largely destroyed, but it was thankfully soon rebuilt owing largely to a successful connection with King Charles I. The church still stands on the old foundation. Most of Keynsham, however, is relatively new, and the town has expanded rapidly over the last few years.

But not only are there old things and new things in Keynsham, there are also things that pass man's understanding if I am to believe old Ted, with whom I had a drink in the Crown inn on the Bristol road. I had been telling Ted over a drink how I had been travelling the area all day in search of haunted houses, ghosts, or at least something unusual, when he said, 'Unusual? Unusual things?' He then went on after a while, 'I could tell you something unusual that recently happened in Keynsham, which I think you, as a stranger, will find hard to believe.'

'Try me,' I said.

'Well, have you ever heard of a haunted chapel or church? I am not talking about such incidents which may occur when one has been alone in a church some late evening, frightened out of one's life, completely horrified, imagining, just because one has heard a little crack in the woodwork, or a noise from the rafters, that the place was haunted, and one was being watched by an untold multitude of unseen faces. We have all experienced something like that in our time. But such imaginings are purely subjective . . . something in your own mind.

'I remember talking with a parson once who admitted being frightened when alone in his own church one night. He remembered in the middle of the night that he had left the door of his vestry unlocked, in which was placed very valuable silver. Unable to sleep he went to investigate. To switch on the lights in his church meant going to unlock a small cupboard, but since it was a moonlit night, and he knew every nook and cranny of the church, he did not think it worthwhile to bother. He was walking down the nave, in the direction of the vestry, humming softly to himself, when he was suddenly convinced he was being followed. He stopped. But who could be out at this time of night, he asked himself, and in any case what would they want of him? He cast it from his mind. To give the impression he was not in the least frightened, he stopped again and looked up at the roof of the church as if he were studying some object. The church was as still as a graveyard . . . so still . . . he was now convinced he could hear someone breathing, as clearly as he could hear his own heart pounding against his ribs. However, not to be intimidated, he began walking on once more, when, to the accompaniment of a torch being switched on, he heard a voice say, "Good evening, Vicar, whatever are you doing here at this time of night?" It was the local policeman!

'No, I am not referring to that sort of thing. I am referring to a haunted chapel or church where things really happened in the night, whether anyone was there or not. Now, I am misleading you a little,' he went on to say, 'because this building was not haunted while it was a place of worship. Unusual things did not really happen until the chapel had been sold.

'It was like this. There was once a chapel in Keynsham, quite a big one with a balcony, one of the Nonconformist group . . . Baptist chapel? Elim? Zion? No, no, no, I think it was known as Bethesda, and was built in the middle of the last century. For a great many years it had flourished and boasted big congregations, until Keynsham itself began to expand into an industrial town. The people living near the chapel began to leave as the land gave way to shops and offices that were rapidly being built. And as the commercial premises expanded, so the congregation of the chapel gradually diminished. Soon it became obvious the chapel would have to be sold. This was especially harrowing for those relatives whose fathers, mothers, sisters and brothers had been buried in the little churchyard in front of the building.

'However, to cut a long story short, the chapel was eventually sold; the road in front of the chapel was widened, and rather than exhume all the bodies in the churchyard, a concrete foundation was laid over the burial ground and paving slabs put into position on top, which, if I may say, made the area look quite attractive and neat. However, it was now no longer a burial ground, but a footpath for shoppers.

'The transition from a place of worship to a secular building took place smoothly enough and very soon the former Bethesda chapel had become a DIY store, clean, sparkling and eager for business.

'It was then that it started, slowly at first, very slowly. A mirror was broken during the night. "Well, who could have done that?" asked the incredulous staff as they arrived in the morning. Investigations were made among the staff, all of whom pleaded, "Not guilty". A few nights after that, paint was spilled on the floor. More questions were asked and investigations began in real earnest. The mirror could have been an accident caused by the wind or the banging of a door, but not this. Paint cannot spill itself all over the floor. Every door and window was examined, and although they did not appear to have been tampered with, more secure locks were fitted. But the vandalism continued. Each morning something else had been broken: wood smashed; wallpaper torn to shreds; nails strewn all over the floor. It just couldn't go on. Employees were becoming distraught and beginning to leave, while people in the town were beginning to talk in knowledgeable terms. "They never should have converted the place," they said. "They shouldn't use these churches for other purposes, should they? And what about all those people who were buried there in the churchyard? Surely the place is being haunted by them"

'However ridiculous their arguments may appear to have been, there were no doubts in the minds of many people that the breakages and curious happenings were not being wrought by human agency.

'After months of doubt the directors, whether they believed in ghosts or not, eventually had the place exorcized, after which the vandalism ceased. However, the workers admitted there was still an uncanny feeling about the place. At one spot in particular, near where the pulpit once stood, it was always cold and clammy, even in the height of summer. There was an inexplicable "something" that caused the place to be particularly uninviting. It was as though there was always someone there in the background . . . some lurking presence that resented the change that had come over the building.'

My friend seemed to have come to the end of his story. I thanked him for telling me and giving me his time, and added, 'Do you believe in ghosts?'

'Well, I never did,' he said, 'but you can't get away from this one, everybody knows about it.' And in answer to my query, he told me where the old Bethesda chapel stood.

I went to see it. The DIY firm had gone. The new people sold carpets. The boss was not in when I called, but his wife was.

'Glorious weather,' I said to her as I opened the door, 'and how hot it is.'

'It's never hot in here,' she said. 'It's always cold!'

The Haunted Gateway

On the A36 Warminster–Bath road, immediately opposite a signpost pointing in the direction of Freshford, there is a drive with a lodge beside it. This is the entrance to Hinton Charterhouse Priory.

The Carthusian Order of Monks who lived here gave the name Charterhouse to their monastic settlement when the second Carthusian home in the country was founded here in 1232. It was founded by the Countess of Salisbury. On the death of her father when she was only seven, Ela, the Countess of Salisbury inherited a large fortune. When her husband, William Longsword, was fighting for his country in the wars against France, news came that he had been killed, and many affluent and attractive young men sought Ela's hand in marriage. However, woman's intuition or premonition persuaded her that her husband was still alive, and consequently she refused them all. Her conviction was well-founded, for he did return home, only to die soon after, and become the first man to be buried in Salisbury Cathedral. When Ela's son had reached the age of maturity, she then went quickly and

Hinton Charterhouse Priory, founded by Ela, the Countess of Salisbury in the thirteenth century

resignedly into a convent, eventually founding the abbey at Lacock in Wiltshire where she became its abbess and eventually died, but not before she had founded Hinton Priory.

Today the priory is scheduled as a national monument. The thirteenth-century chapter house, with the library and sacristy, survive, and excavations have revealed the simple little church, with small houses around it, where the monks (there were never more than twelve) resigned themselves to a quiet life of prayer and meditation.

But Hinton Charterhouse has changed over the years. In days gone by there was no lodge there, just wrought-iron gates and, within the gates, lining each side of the stony drive, were elm trees of massive proportions. Massive sculptured pillars supported those gates. The abbey itself, at the end of the drive, was unsighted, as, indeed, it is today.

It is hard to translate into modern terms the things of yesteryear. There could not have been twelve houses within four miles of that road beside which the gates were erected. Hinton itself, where there were a few more houses, was more than a mile away. There were no lights on the highways, and cottages lit by candles were dull compared with the lighted houses of today. No coaches were speeding by; no cars with fierce headlights illumined the roads. At night-time all was dark . . . dark . . . impenetrable blackness.

And yet as dark as it was those great wrought iron gates, with their massive stone supports, stood out so well that they appeared like terrific giants holding a net between them, to take up and crush anyone who dared approach. It is said those gates were haunted, haunted by the dead, so no one ever walked there when the sun was setting behind the trees at eventide. But why should the gates be haunted? And who were the dead who haunted them? No one seems to know. That is the great mystery that shrouds those entrance gates.

I have heard that highwaymen and smugglers in time past composed such stories as I am now telling to keep people inside their homes, so that they could continue their nefarious and sometimes dreadful deeds unwitnessed and undisturbed. But, no highwaymen came this way to plunder and no smugglers trod this path with their ill-gotten gains. Consequently, no one benefitted by talking of haunted gates at an entrance to an abbey on a lonely highway. The story of the haunted gates was not a tale devised to frighten people away. The story was told only because it was true.

At the moment, however, we have only spoken of the gateway at eventide. But at midnight – yes, in the middle of the night – it is said an awful curse hung over those gates, and those who had ever seen them at midnight could well believe it. Why, anyone who wandered near them at midnight, unless they had hearts of steel, was almost certain to suffer from horrible convulsions or die of fright. Yet the real trouble concerning those gates, no one knew and that was the second great mystery that surrounded them.

What was known, however, and well attested was that, as soon as the bell tolled from the belfry tower, the gates would open, apparently of their own volition and gradually at first, as though they were being held back by a mighty force. And as they moved, strange, eerie noises emanated from the huge stone supports. And always it was to let someone enter, for almost instantaneously a loud sound of horses dragging a heavy coach could be heard. On other occasions voices of many people could be heard passing through, echoing and re-echoing as if in danger or distress. And then, as the noises slowly died away on the wind, the gates would ponderously close again.

It is almost impossible today to state accurately where those gates stood, and therefore who it was who drove through them. That is the third great mystery. Yet, there is no doubt that what I have told you is an established fact that has been spoken of down the ages. Perhaps some day, one day, those mysteries may be solved. Who knows?

13: Stranger Than Fiction

The Blind Fiddler. The Clever Oxen. Theophilus Brome. The Wedding.

The Blind Fiddler

The tiny medieval church of Thurloxton, near Taunton, with its seventeenth-century screen and pulpit, and Norman font, once contained a curious relic in the tower, in the shape of a wooden leg. I would like to tell you about it.

On board his own ship during the Battle of Copenhagen on 2 April 1801, Viscount Admiral Horatio Nelson (1758–1805), spoke the following and now immortal words:

> It is warm work; and the day may be the last to any of us at a moment. But mark you! I would not be elsewhere for thousands.

It had been warm work. It had also been hard work. Many on board that ship were suffering from weariness, pain and depression. Food was short, sleep almost impossible and many were at the point of death.

There were but three people on that ship who made life a little more tolerable, and offered some hope for the future. The first was Horatio Nelson himself, whose courage, tenacity and

Thurloxton church, where a curious relic was kept in the tower

purpose in the presence of great odds, kept the fit on their toes; the less fit, the more determined; and those who suffered pain and loneliness, hopeful that right would prevail in the end, and they would be saved.

The second was the chaplain, who was tireless in his devotion to everyone on the ship, especially to those who were suffering pain and conflict through no fault of their own. And the third was an old blind fiddler who exuded faith and hope in whatever he did.

The chaplain was especially mindful of the old blind fiddler, who had lost a leg while saving him from the jaws of death at the Battle of Cape St Vincent some four years before. And then, following the chaplain because of his devotion to him, he was blinded in the subsequent Battle of Copenhagen. In pain and anguish the now blinded wooden-legged man constantly played his violin, generally to keep up the spirits of the other men on board, but equally, if not more so, to keep the cries of the suffering from the men who were fighting.

After the Battle of Copenhagen, the chaplain retired from the Navy and settled down as Rector of Thurloxton, a village not far from Taunton. For years, he performed his duty as rector of the little village with the same undivided loyalty he had shown as chaplain in the Navy. Not only did the people in the village love him, but strangers and beggars who were passing soon began to recognize him as their friend and saviour. Very soon his rectory became an open house for all who cared to call.

One winter evening, when rain was teeming down and the wind blowing a gale, and the rector was particularly pleased that he had no cause to leave his warm, sequestered rectory, there was a knock on the door. He waited awhile, for surely no one could be knocking on his door at that hour on such a beastly night. But the knock was repeated. Slowly he went to the door. There on the doorstep he could see the outline of a man, nothing more, who asked for a lodging till the morning, 'for the night is beastly,' he said, 'and I am hungry and can go no further'.

When the man had entered into the light of the candle-lit room and the glow of the fire, the rector noticed that he carried a bag containing an old violin, and that his visitor was not only lame, but also had to be led to a chair beside the fire, as though the light of the room momentarily blinded his sight. The rector also noticed he was exhausted, and within a few moments he was asleep and dead to the world.

As the rector began to remove the man's wet clothes and gently rub him down he noticed that his lameness was due to the fact that he had a wooden leg, and on a closer and more thorough inspection, he became convinced that the man was the old blind fiddler, who, many years ago, had saved him from death.

Yet, how could a blind man have found his house in this out-of-the-way village of Thurloxton? Did the old blind fiddler know that he was knocking at the door of his old chaplain? Where had he been during the intervening years? These were the questions the rector asked himself as he gazed intently at the man across the fire . . . the old blind fiddler who had followed him from ship to ship with an endearing devotion that knew no bounds. He would have liked to have fetched the doctor to him immediately, for he was well aware that the old man needed one, but he dared not leave him in case he should awake and find himself alone. The doctor would have to wait until the morning.

The rectory at Thurloxton, perhaps still haunted by the ghost of the old blind fiddler

When the doctor arrived next day the rector was told that the old blind fiddler was desperately ill and would either have to be taken to the nearest workhouse or have a bed in the rector's home. The rector immediately decided on the latter.

Between the warm sheets in a bed in the rector's home the old man began to revive, but only sufficiently to assure the rector he had fought in both the Battle of Cape St Vincent and the Battle of Copenhagen, and had lost a leg in one, and his eyesight in the other. There was no doubt that the traveller was the old blind fiddler who had saved the rector from a premature death.

One day, after he had been in bed for some four weeks without any sign of improvement in his condition, he asked the rector for his old violin. These were the first words he had uttered since telling his host of his past adventures when he first arrived, for the rest of the rector's queries in the intervening period had been merely acknowledged by a nod of the head.

Fondling his violin, his constant companion, and tucking it under his chin, the old man began to play 'so well,' the rector maintained, 'that he had never heard the violin played so movingly before.' The music filled the whole of that gaunt old rectory as though the violin were being played for him by an administering spirit. It was indeed what one might describe as heavenly music. With his face wreathed in an enchanting smile the old blind fiddler handed the violin back to the rector, sank immediately into the pillows, and was wafted into eternity.

After the funeral the rector had the old fiddler's wooden leg placed in the tower of the church, where it remained for many years.

A few weeks after the demise of the old man the rector began to hear strange tappings coming from the bedroom where the blind fiddler had passed away. For a long time he endeavoured to ascertain the cause of the tappings, for he never remembered hearing them in days gone by. He finally became convinced they were caused by the wooden leg, as the old fiddler's ghost walked abroad in the rectory, chiefly when darkness was enveloping the land. The tappings never worried the rector in the slightest. He had always lived on his own and consequently, whenever he heard the strange sounds, he became convinced it was the old fiddler, coming back from the dead, to offer him company in the rectory, in exchange for the company that had been offered him in his last days on this earth.

It is said that these strange tappings are heard even today, but whether that is so, I cannot say.

The Clever Oxen

Montacute, a village on the A3088 Yeovil–South Petherton road, boasts the greatest mansion and the finest specimen of Elizabethan architecture in Somerset. But the village itself is also of great interest. It was known, at one time, by the name of Leodgaresburgh until the Normans came, who changed it to Montacute, said to have been derived from the sharp pointed St Michael's Hill: Mons Acutus.

According to a twelfth-century manuscript, a blacksmith of the village of Leodgaresburgh dreamed on three occasions that Christ appeared to him, beseeching him to take the priest and some men to the top of St Michael's Hill and dig. It was, by the way, on the top of this hill that William the Conqueror's brother, the Earl of Morteign, built a castle, and it was his son who founded the Cluniac Priory at its foot. Twice the blacksmith disregarded the dream, but on the third occasion, he told the priest about it. Subsequently the blacksmith, the priest and some villagers climbed the hill and began digging. Eventually, they came upon a great stone which miraculously split in two, and in the cleft they saw a great crucifix of glistening black flint. Beneath it was a smaller one, an old bell and an old book.

Now the proud and powerful Dane, Tofig, who was King Canute's standard-bearer, had for a long time been anxious to build a minster at Waltham in Essex, where he had great possessions. Hearing of the discovery of the crucifix he came with all haste to Leodgaresburgh. He told all and sundry that he wished to take it away immediately, for this was the crucifix, he said, around which he would love to build his abbey.

However, he had not reckoned with the people of Somerset. They did not particularly want to part with the 'wonder working' cross, as it was subsequently called, and much discussion took place between the two camps. Finally Tofig devised a scheme.

He placed the great crucifix, with the smaller cross and the book and bell on a new cart drawn by twelve red oxen. Then to be fair to everyone concerned, he said he would call out places of great historical and spiritual interest, and let the oxen decide for themselves where the crucifix should go. Of course Tofig himself wished the oxen to make the long journey to Essex. The oxen at first seemed to side with the men of Somerset, for they did not appear to want to bear away the crucifix. Tofig mentioned Canterbury, but the oxen did not move. Glastonbury was tried, but they did not stir. Other shrines were mentioned to no purpose, but then, when Waltham was mentioned, the oxen started off briskly.

How long it took them to get to Waltham, we do not know. But we do know the crucifix reached Waltham, and over the high altar of the abbey Tofig set up the Cross of Montacute. It is said that when Harold, king of the Saxons, looked up at the crucifix, it bowed down to him, which inspired the English to cry 'Holy Cross' as they went into battle. Furthermore, such was their faith that they were for a time victorious, until their enthusiasm caused them to break ranks, with the result that King Harold was slain by the Normans.

THEOPHILUS BROME

Inside the church of Chilton Cantelo, a hamlet within a few miles of Sparkford on the A395 road, lies the body of Theophilus Brome.

Now Theophilus Brome was one of those unfortunate people who lived during the ferocious period of the seventeenth century, when there were uprisings between the Church and State, between the Church and Puritanism, and King James II and Monmouth. It was indeed hard to sit on the fence. One had to come down on one side or the other.

During the Civil War, 1645, Theophilus Brome had to make the decision of his life. Although he was a devout and loyal Englishman, he finally came down on the side of the Parliamentarians in opposition to the Crown, simply because he opposed some of the cruelty he had heard emanated from the Royalists, and which, indeed, he himself had witnessed. He therefore found himself fighting on the side of the Parliamentarians, although he must have known the Parliamentarians were capable of similar acts of barbarity. However, he could not erase from his mind having seen the Royalists, hanging the enemy and impaling their heads on railings and making sport of the whole affair. It revolted him.

He was not a traitor: he was a nationalist; an Englishman; a true gentleman; and he loved his country. But he abominated cruelty, and what he had seen had such an effect upon him that his one abiding fear was having his own head exhibited on a spike for public exhibition.

Now the inscription on his tomb suggests that he lived in the county of Warwickshire, but his sister lived here in the little

Higher Farm, Chilton Cantelo where Theophilus Brome sought refuge during the Civil War

village of Chilton Cantelo in the house now called Higher Farm. When Theophilus was wounded, in order to avoid the Royalists, he had settled here in this house opposite the church. He felt that this little out-of-the-way place was unlikely to be discovered by the Royalists.

Although he had seen the end of the Civil War and an uncertain peace descend on the land, and the restoration to the throne of King Charles II in 1660, Theophilus Brome could not rid himself of the sight of those poor helpless soldiers being impaled for all to see. This memory impressed itself upon his mind the more so when he realized that the wounds he had received in the Civil War, all those many years ago, were gradually taking away his life.

Before he died, therefore, he had three requests to make: he pleaded with his sister to have his head separated from his body, so that even if his body were discovered by any warring faction in the future, his head would not be impaled; he wished to have his head deposited in his sister's house where he hoped it would be allowed to remain for ever; and finally he asked that the other part of his body be buried in the church of St James in Chilton Cantelo. All these requests were granted.

I was indeed very fortunate when I called on Mr and Mrs Charles Kerton to ask whether I might be allowed to see the skull of Mr Theophilus Brome. There, in the hall of their lovely home, was a securely locked, elongated, black oak cupboard hanging on the wall. Inside this cupboard was the skull of Theophilus Brome, beside which was a stiff cardbord cover containing fragments of a will dated 1690 of a William Brome, who asked to be buried at the discretion of Miss Lettice Brome, the sister of Theophilus. There was also a brief history of the Brome family. We gather from the will that Miss Lettice Brome eventually married Thomas Edes, an apothecary from Warwick.

Now I am almost convinced that the majority of people reading the story of Theophilus Brome will have reached the conclusion that not everyone who had lived at Higher Farm since 1670 would have been a relative of the Brome family. Therefore it was obvious they would not wish this skull to remain in their home. Surely they would have had it removed and interred elsewhere, and especially as the churchyard was only across the road? Yet, in some peculiar way, plans for its removal have never been carried out.

When I first heard this story, my first reaction was to read what Collinson the Somerset historian had to say on the subject. He writes:

> There is a tradition in the parish that the person here interred inside the church, requested that his head might be taken off before his burial and be preserved at the Farm House near the church, where his head, chop-fallen enough, is still shown . . . which the tenants of the house have often endeavoured to commit to the bowels of the earth, but have been so often deterred by horrid noises, portentive of sad displeasure; and about 20 years since (which was perhaps the last attempt) the sexton, in digging a place for the skull's repository, broke his spade in two places, and uttered a solemn affirmation never more to attempt an act, evidently repugnant to the quiet of Brome's head.

So Theophilus's body has remained quiet and peaceful in the church of Chilton Cantelo since 1670. Even when they built a new church in Victorian times on the old foundations, his grave was undisturbed. His epitaph maintains that he died in peace, and it appears that the world has allowed him to continue in that vein, just as the epitaph puts it: at peace with the world, and true to his friends. His head, meanwhile, remains in the beautiful home of Higher Farm as he requested in 1670. It is a remarkable thing, is it not, that it has never been removed and interred elsewhere, as I am convinced many residents of Higher Farm would have wished.

Mrs Kerton told me that before she married the present owner of Higher Farm, she visited the house one evening to call on her future husband and was understandably somewhat perturbed about living in the same house with Theophilus Brome following the marriage. On that moonlit night, when she was about to leave and get into her car, her future husband, seeing what he thought was a black shadow on the ground, shouted to her that she had dropped her coat in the courtyard. The shadow was not her coat. It was the top of the well, which she must have missed by only a few inches. But there was no cover on the well. Who had removed it? And who had been so careless not to have replaced it? Was it that Theophilus was fearful that Mrs Kerton, the future lady of Higher Farm, would have his skull removed? Who knows?

On another occasion the present owner's father, having invited friends to the house especially to see the skull, put his silver tobacco case into the pocket of his dinner jacket with a view to offering tobacco to his friends when, and if, the occasion arose. However, later that evening, when he put his hand in his pocket, the expensive case was missing. A diligent search of all his pockets, and the house, was made without success. The next time he wore his dinner jacket the case was found in his pocket.

The comedian Dave Allen and a friend, so I was told by Mrs Kerton, visited Higher Farm to see the skull. I hope they didn't make fun of it. But certainly on their way home, when the friend of Dave Allen struck a match to light a cigarette, it broke in half and the lighted end fell in to the turn-up of his trousers, destroying his suit.

Mr Kerton told me that a few years ago he decided to re-decorate the extensive hall, which is where the cupboard housing the skull is situated. In the middle of the night, when both Mr and Mrs Kerton were in bed, they heard a tremendous crash in the hall below. On examination it was found that the barometer, which had always hung in the hall, had crashed onto the stone floor, landing up against the wall opposite. But the glass and mercury were still intact, and the only damage to the frame was so small, it was hardly noticeable. When I asked Mr Kerton why he thought the barometer had crashed, it was his belief, he said, that Theophilus did not like to be disturbed.

Undoubtedly there are probable and simple explanations for all these occurrences, including the sexton's spade mentioned by Collinson. Although one has to admit the experiences are peculiar, they are certainly no more remarkable than the fact that the skull of Theophilus Brome has remained in that house for three hundred years.

I wonder what would happen if someone was definitely determined to remove the skull once and for all? I hope no one ever tries.

The Wedding

Beside the River Chew at Stanton Drew, to which I have already referred, you will see some enormous stones (a miniature Stonehenge) about which, obviously, there is much conjecture. These stones are known as 'The Great Circle', and it is said that twenty-seven of the original thirty stones survive. There is 'The Cove' beside the 'Druids Arms', comprising three

The three great stones of 'The Cove' at Stanton Drew, in 1723

great stones. There is a single stone which we have already seen, known as 'Hautville's Quoit', and two other stones known as 'Middle Ham', all forming a complex of a mile across. Some people refer to 'The Great Circle' (similar to Stonehenge and Avebury) as a crude temple of the Ancient Britons. Certain folk maintain that the stones have nothing whatever to do with sun worship, and neither are they very old. Others declare, while looking at the 'Druids Arms', that the 'Drew' in Stanton Drew refers to the Druids, who, they believe, erected the stones, while some affirm that Drew is a family name of the Drew or Drogo family who once owned considerable land in the district. But many will tell you that these are no more than theories or suppositions, and that the real answer lies elsewhere. Let me explain.

Hundreds of years ago, on a glorious Saturday evening in August, a wedding was solemnized in the parish church of Stanton Drew. After the service the bride and groom and the guests retired to the local barn and partook of a sumptuous meal, accompanied by considerable supplies of cider. Much later in the evening most of the guests repaired to the field beside the river, just beyond the church, to dance. After quite a while, when many of the guests and the musicians were retiring towards midnight, the master of ceremonies suggested that all should do so, for the Sabbath was now approaching. However, there were some in that company, very few it must be said, who were in favour of dancing on into the Sabbath, for what harm might it do? However, the musicians had definitely decided that the next dance was to be the last. As they began to walk away across the field, a stranger appeared in the midst of those guests who were anxious to continue dancing. The stranger, smiling in a most attractive way, said he would be quite willing to accompany the dancing be it Sabbath or not, if they sincerely wished to continue. They asked him to prove his ability so, taking up the violin, he played with such inspiration and vivacity that it imbued many, who were in the process of leaving, with the desire to stay and dance.

So vivid was the music, so alive and virile, so enchanting and enthralling, that within a few minutes the bride and groom, and those guests who had stayed, were under the musician's spell. And it is said, by those who had decided to go home, that the music of the violin could be heard across the vale, echoing and re-echoing its song.

Next morning, all that was left in the field were stones. It is said that it was the devil who had produced that lively and compelling music, and so enraptured were the dancers by him that they were unconsciously calling his tune while he turned them one and all into stone.

Local people will tell you that the stones known as 'The Cove', near the 'Druids Arms', are the parson, bride and groom; the larger circle, the dancers; and the small circle, the musicians, who had returned to hear the fiddler.

It must have been an exciting night.

14: Love Stories

The Prior's Love. Jilted Love. Love at First Sight.

The Prior's Love

Matthew, the prior, was not an ornithologist in the accepted sense of the word, although he did like to walk beside the river, watch the birds in flight, the movement of the fish and the

Muchelney Abbey, the fifteenth-century abbey where Matthew, the prior lived with the ever-constant memory of his love, Drusilla

patience and alertness of the herons. He had always been a man of ordinary longings. In time past he had participated in all kinds of outdoor activities and associated with all kinds of people, until for one reason or the other, he had given up all worldly longings and all human loves. So changed was he, that he had come to live with the other monks in the fifteenth-century Muchelney Abbey.

He was now a changed man and needs like human excitement, longings and ambitions had been put into the back of his mind. His life, since he had come to the monastery, was spent in penitence and tranquility. All he wanted now was to be at peace with God and help those poor, dear souls who had been committed to his charge. He would hear their confessions, give them counsel, and occasionally administer the Blessed Sacrament.

On one occasion, when the world seemed at peace as he walked along the river bank to the nunnery, his mind went back to those days when he himself used to fish, hunt, climb and row, and as he reminisced so he remembered the young lady with whom he had once fallen deeply in love and with whom he had joined in those worldly pursuits. That such a sensation should come to him at that particular moment was peculiar, for he thought he had been able to cast such things from his mind altogether. As he walked slowly along the banks of the river he seemed almost to be in the presence of that young lady, and could even hear her speaking to him. He was annoyed, for he had done all he could to rid himself of thoughts of bygone days. He shook himself vigorously from his lethargy and began to walk faster in an endeavour to drive all such thoughts from his mind until he reached the home of the sisterhood it was his duty to serve, where he knew he would be too busy to think of things of yesteryear.

His duty that particular day was to give a short address and to listen to, and if possible, answer the sisters' questions and, if the occasion arose, make an appropriate time to hear their confessions. He listened for quite a while to their individual problems, for young ladies in confined religious communities are not immune from these. He answered them all one by one.

But as he was approaching the end of his time, one sister was persistent in asking questions which seemed very different from the rest. She was worried, she said, for God was so often blotted out during her meditations by the love she once had for a young man she had lost. 'This person,' she said, 'comes before me and blots out God; what must I do?'

'What is this,' he asked himself, 'Am I really hearing this or is it a figment of my imagination? This is surely the sort of thing about which she should be talking to her Mother Superior, not to me.'

The prior should not have listened any more to the distressed female and yet he wanted to for, on that particular day, it was music to his ears. His heart began to beat as it had done before he entered the fraternity. His mind went back to the sweet girl he had known, with blue eyes, lilting voice and pleasant song. It all came back to him like a dream one remembers on awakening.

Oh, if only he had left at that moment, or told the sister in question to talk to her Mother Superior. But he couldn't. Curiosity had got the better of him, and he must delve more into the young sister's heart and mind.

'Tell me, Sister,' he asked, 'what is your name, where did you live, and who is it who troubles you?'

'My name is Drusilla,' she answered without hesitation. 'Before I came to the sisterhood I lived in Cornwall, and he who troubles me is Matthew, whom I knew when I was young. But then,' she said, 'ah, then . . . his father chose for him a richer bride, and I was left heartbroken and alone. Finally I sought shelter in this sisterhood, and although I have tried my utmost to drive him from my mind, and done my duty here, yet he who once owned my love comes through my prayers, my singing, and my thoughts.'

'It is Drusilla,' thought the prior to himself. But then, in a loud and authoritative manner he said, 'I must hear no more. I must go. You, Sister, should talk to your Mother Superior, or I will do it for you, if you wish.'

There was a deathly hush. The other sisters rose one by one and departed, and as Sister Drusilla passed through the door, she looked back to get a glimpse of the prior, and their eyes met. When Matthew returned to the monastery that day he asked the abbot whether he might be relieved of his duty at the nunnery. He felt he wanted a change, he said.

For some twelve months he never entered the door of the nunnery again, although his heart missed a beat whenever he thought of the last time he went, and the angry way he had stopped the proceedings. He was sorry when he thought of it, for undoubtedly the sister was the same Drusilla he had known in his younger days of whom his father had not approved, because he had wished his son to marry the daughter of a friend. Because Matthew felt he could not obey his father's wishes, but yet did not wish to hurt him, he decided to separate himself from his father and the world. The only love he ever knew was Drusilla with whom he had grown up, and loved with all his heart. There was no other person he could love.

From the moment the prior ceased to visit the nunnery Drusilla had been broken-hearted. She could not erase from her mind the authoritative way in which the prior had finished his session. Days and weeks went by, and the more he absented himself, the more she became depressed. Her old liveliness began to ebb, her pulse began to beat slower, and life, it seemed, was beginning to leave those heavenly blue eyes. She could not understand why God had treated her so. Surely, she thought, it could not be wrong to say what was in her thoughts, for that is all she had done. Why was God treating her this way? Why?

As the months went by Drusilla became weaker and weaker for no explicable reason, for physically, opined the Mother Superior, there was nothing wrong with her.

Thirteen weary months went by before the abbot once more requested Matthew to go to the nunnery, for the other brother was ill. 'While you are there,' the abbot continued, 'will you please go to see one of the sisters who I have been told is very ill.' Then he added, as if as an afterthought, 'and it may be advisable to take the sacrament with you.'

Although Matthew could not refuse, his mind was so unsettled that he knew not what to do. He knew he was not in the right frame of mind to hear the sisters' confessions, yet, as a good parish priest, he did so and gave them absolution. But where was Drusilla? Why did she not come? Surely she had not left the nunnery? But then, as if in answer to these questions, the Mother Superior said, 'Would you come in here to administer the sacrament to one of my sisters? She does not seem to get stronger, or possess the will to live, and I can only think she is dying. There is the room,' she said, pointing.

Matthew went into the sister's little room, only to see the wasted form of Drusilla, and for a moment, which seemed an eternity, he felt all virtue drain from him. She looked up to him as he entered, and, realizing it was Matthew, sat up as though to fling herself into his arms, but her failing strength prevented her and she collapsed into her bed. After a moment she smiled, which meant everything in the world to Matthew, and for a passing moment life came back to those heavenly blue eyes. 'Matthew,' she said, 'do please forgive me, I know it is you – and I do love you still.'

The prior was pleased that the Mother Superior had not come into the little room with him, but as soon as she did he gave Drusilla absolution and the Blessed Sacrament, and then asked the Mother Superior to leave them for a moment.

In that brief moment, he stooped down to her, and said, 'I forgive you, my Drusilla and I STILL love you.' He then placed his hand on her forehead and blessed her, and then kissed her tenderly on her lips. Opening her eyes once more, she smiled, and closing them again was wafted into eternity. And as Matthew closed her eyelids; a little tear fell slowly down her cheek. The monks buried her a few days afterwards with much chanting and weeping. Matthew saw the little grave, placed a lone flower upon it and then went, unnoticed in the dark, back to his cell.

Years afterwards, within that little cell, Matthew passed away. He had been a good prior, although he had kept himself to himself for many years. His only belongings were a crucifix and a Bible. The monks placed the crucifix in his right hand, and the Bible they placed in his left. There was nothing inside the Bible apart from a few hand-written words on the inside cover. They were: 'I love you Drusilla; Drusilla, my love'.

None of the monks ever knew what it meant or to whom it referred.

JILTED LOVE

The glory of Backwell, a big and progressive village on the A370 road from Weston-super-Mare to Bristol, lies not in its main street, but in its hills to the south, where there are three enchanting combes beyond the magnificent eleventh-century church of St Andrew. The church is at the centre of the old part of the village, as it was before Backwell expanded, and beside it is the old manor, the home of the Rodney family from the twelfth to the seventeenth century.

A very touching story concerns a part of the church that had been hidden for ages. In 1933 a wall was pulled down in the church revealing Sir Walter Rodney, Kt, lying recumbent in an exquisite chapel, which Elizabeth Rodney, out of love and consideration for him, had built in his memory. Furthermore, we learn that after Walter's death in 1460, although Elizabeth had married again, she was finally brought back to lie by Walter Rodney's side in the chapel, which she had had surrounded by a host of angels.

But to show to what lengths true love will go I must tell you about the last of the Rodneys to live in the manor beside the church. The most touching incident to which I refer concerns Sir George Rodney who fell in love with a young widow, the daughter of Viscount Howard of Bindon. However, I am afraid she did not return his love and to make matters worse, she married a much more elderly gentleman, the Earl of Hertford.

Broken-hearted, Sir George followed her to an inn at Amesbury, locked himself in a room, and there wrote her a poem of 140 verses, in his own blood, and then, like a true warrior, fell upon his sword.

It is said that when an inventory was taken of all his goods, there was one sword among them, which was worth 6s. 8d. That was the end: the end of love for Sir George; the end of the Backwell Rodneys.

Love at First Sight

I had come to Weston, not Weston-super-Mare but the Weston near Bath, which to avoid confusion is now frequently called Weston-Bath, to see a memorial to Sir Charles Frankland. This had been placed in the church by his affectionate widow, Agnes, about whom there is quite a remarkable story.

I was indeed disappointed and amazed to find there was no mention of either Sir Charles Frankland or Agnes (Lady Frankland) in a booklet, *Looking back at Weston, (1535–1900)*, and it was only through the industry of Mr and Mrs Brain, of 9 Church Road, that I eventually found the memorial.

Sir Charles Frankland, a descendent of Cromwell through his youngest daughter Frances, after inheriting a fortune went to settle in Massachusetts, where he became known as a scholar and a connoisseur, if not an eccentric.

On one occasion, while staying at an inn, he saw a bare-footed but beautiful maid of about sixteen by the name of Agnes Surriage, scrubbing stairs in the inn. He became infatuated by her. Within days, thinking, undoubtedly because of his rank, he had every right to do so, he took her away and had her educated by a puritan minister, which enabled her to administer, with a degree of elegance and propriety, an estate which he subsequently acquired.

However, at the age of thirty-one, Frankland had to return to England to succeed his uncle to the baronetcy, and during his stay he was successful in winning a legal battle for the family estate in Yorkshire. To celebrate his victory and the fortune he had procured, he took Agnes away on a tour of Europe which had remarkable consequences. While he was staying in Lisbon, there was an appalling earthquake in which 30,000 people lost their lives and half the city was destroyed. Frankland's carriage, in which he had been travelling to church accompanied by a young lady (not Agnes), was smashed to smithereens and the horses killed.

After the earthquake had stopped, but with the streets still unsafe, Agnes, who had remained at home, went out in a desperate search for Frankland and miraculously found him, at the point of death, beneath a heap of fallen masonry which had pinioned him for hours. After rescuing him, Agnes dressed his wounds and immediately sent for a priest who took the opportunity to marry them. Frankland soon recovered and since his dwelling had been destroyed, he and Agnes, now, of course, Lady Frankland, embarked once more for England where she was royally welcomed wherever she went.

Two years later they again made their home in Lisbon, after Sir Charles had been appointed Consul for Portugal. Within two years, however, Agnes became so homesick for New England that he found it imperative to quit his employ, enabling both to set out for America where they stayed for some time. Finally returning to England at the request of Sir Charles, whose health was gradually failing him, they spent their last happy months together in Weston-Bath, where he died in 1768.

After a short time the old desire for America reawakened itself in Agnes, and once more she found herself on American soil where she not only witnessed the Battle of Bunkers Hill, but helped to dress the wounds of those who fought in that savage battle. Even so, being the widow of an officer of the English Crown, Agnes was not wholly accepted in America as she would have been before the War of Independence. Consequently this beautiful young girl, who at one time scrubbed steps in Massachusetts, returned to England once more, where she later married a banker at Chichester, and where she is commemorated by a monument in the cathedral.

15: Wills

No Snivelling at his Funeral. Oliver's Whelp. The Querulous Daughters.

NO SNIVELLING AT HIS FUNERAL

Running alongside the church in Weston-Bath is Purlewent Road. Samuel Purlewent, who died on 30 July 1792, was an attorney of great professional esteem, and it was due to this fact, and that he was an outstanding personality, that the road

Weston-Bath church where the eminent eighteenth-century attorney Samuel Purlewent requested to be buried

was named after him. Although for years he resided at Lincoln's Inn, where he died, he expressed a wish to be buried in Weston-Bath. His will, which I now quote, is of unusual interest:

> Samuel Purlewent, late of Lincoln's Inn, in the County of Middlesex, Esq, deceased, proved November 19th, 1792. It is my express will and desire that I may be buried at Weston, in the County of Somerset if I die there, if not, to be carried down there (but not in a hearse) nor will I have any parade or coach to attend upon me, but let me be carried in any vehicle, with all the expedition possible to Weston so as the same do not exceed £25, and when I arrive there, I direct six poor people of Weston, do support my corpse to the grave, and that six poor women and six poor men of Weston do attend me to the grave and that I may be buried at Twelve at Noon, and each of them do have half a guinea; and I hereby

The Crown Inn where Samuel Purlewent decreed that a sumptuous meal be provided after his death

order and direct, that a good boiled ham, a dozen fowls, a sirloin of beef, with plum puddings may be provided at the 'Crown' in Weston, for the said eighteen poor people besides the clerk and sexton. And I allow five guineas for the same: and I request and hope that they will be as merry as possible, for I consider it a mere farce to put on the grimace of weeping, crying, snivelling and the like, which can answer no good end, either to the living or dead and which I reprobate on the highest terms.

CODICIL

I desire that after I am buried, there be a cool collation provided at the public house, a sirloin of beef, potatoes, and a fillet of veal, with plenty of good ale, where I hope they will refresh themselves with decency and propriety. No friends or relations whatever do attend my funeral.

Oliver's Whelp

Although Wincanton is a modern town, since it was nearly all destroyed by fire in 1707, history tells us that the Romans settled here long ago. Here the first blood of the 1688 revolution was spilled when William of Orange, on his way to London, put to rout a party of Royalists.

John Langley, one of Cromwell's Ironsides who was born at Wincanton, appears to have been a self-opinionated man, not easily put out by adversaries, or forgiving to those who had scorned him during his life. When he died in Ireland during the Commonwealth, many people had a shock when they heard his will read. I do not expect it will shock you in the same way, but I do think you may find it of interest. Here it is:

I, John Langley, born in Wincanton in Somersetshire, and settled in Ireland in the year 1651, now in my right mind and wits, do make my Will in my own handwriting. I do leave all my house, goods and farm of Black Kettle, of 253 acres to my son, commonly called 'Stubborn Jack,' to him and his heirs forever, provided he marries a Protestant, But not Alice Kendrick, who called me 'Oliver's Whelp'. My new buckskin breeches and silver tobacco stopper with J.L. on the top, I give to Richard, my comrade, who helped me off at the storming of Clonmel, when I was shot through the leg. My said son John, shall keep my body above ground six days and six nights after I am dead, and Grace Kendrick shall lay me out, who shall have for so doing five shillings. My body shall be put on the oak table in the brown room, and fifty Irishmen shall be invited to my Wake, and everyone shall have two quarts of the aqua vitae, and each one skin, dish, and knife before him; and when the liquor is out nail up the coffin and commit me to the earth, whence I came. This is my will, witness this my hand, this 3rd March, 1674.

John Langley

The Querulous Daughters

When first I visited a small village by the name of Kilmersdon, near Stratton-on-the-Fosse, I found it so fascinating that, for a time, I was rooted to the spot. It struck me as a place of great character and dignity. The church tower, some 100 ft high, looked graceful and charming, peeping out of the cluster of trees that formed a kind of amphitheatre around it.

I am told that here is the origin of the nursery rhyme 'Jack and Jill went up the Hill', and where 'Jack fell down and broke his crown'. But whether that is so I cannot prove. But I can prove what the will of one Gabriel Goodman was.

Gabriel Goodman, the lord of the manor of Kilmersdon, had two daughters, and in dealing with them I do not think he was blessed with too much common sense. Although he tried to be guarded in whatever he did, in the matter of his will, he failed lamentably. Here it is:

> I have perused my Will and upon second thoughts see that my household stuff and plate is to be divided between my two daughters and as it is very considerable and of little value and the dividing of it may make some breach between my two daughters, it is my request to you, that be my Executors, that you prevail with my daughter, Mary Goodman, that her sister Sarah Twyford may have it all. If she shall refuse to do this she is very unworthy of what I have done for her. I hope she will comply with my desire. God grant that they may live lovingly as sisters ought to do. And pray do you what in you lies to keep up a good and right understanding between them, and that there may not be any difference between them and that they may live in peace and love, as sisters ought to do. This is the desire and command of their father, if they do obey God's command and I am sure they will grant me this.
>
> Gabriel Goodman.

Poor gullible Gabriel. Or was he? It is said that the sisters became so embroiled in litigation that there was hardly any money left over to enjoy.